Business Ethics & SOCIETY

DANTES/DSST* Test Study Guide

All rights reserved. This Study Guide, Book and Flashcards are protected under the US Copyright Law. No part of this book or study guide or flashcards may be reproduced, distributed or stored in a retrieval system, or transmitted in any form or by any means, electronic, mechanical, photocopying, recording, or otherwise, without the prior written permission of the publisher Breely Crush Publishing, LLC.

© 2026 Breely Crush Publishing, LLC

DSST is a registered trademark of The Thomson Corporation and its affiliated companies, and does not endorse this book.

971010620143

Copyright ©2003 - 2026, Breely Crush Publishing, LLC.

All rights reserved.

This Study Guide, Book and Flashcards are protected under the US Copyright Law. No part of this publication may be reproduced, distributed or stored in a retrieval system, or transmitted in any form or by any means, electronic, mechanical, photocopying, recording, or otherwise, without the prior written permission of the publisher Breely Crush Publishing, LLC.

Published by Breely Crush Publishing, LLC
10808 River Front Parkway
South Jordan, UT 84095
www.breelycrushpublishing.com

ISBN-10: 1-61433-658-X
ISBN-13: 978-1-61433-658-7

Printed and bound in the United States of America.

*DSST is a registered trademark of The Thomson Corporation and its affiliated companies, and does not endorse this book.

Table of Contents

Business Ethics 1
Moral Philosophies & Business Ethics 4
    Fundamentals of Ethics 4
    Kohlberg's Model of Cognitive Moral Development 6
    Consequentialism 9
    Mill's Utilitarianism 10
    Act and Rule Utilitarianism 11
    Deontology 12
    Kantian Ethics 13
    Virtue Ethics 15
    Comparing Ethical Perspectives 15
Social Responsibility 17
Ethics in Information 22
    Marketing 22
    Pricing Strategies 23
    Protecting and Stealing Proprietary Information 25
    Corporate Espionage 27
    Bluffing 29
    Conflicts of Interest 29
    Insider Trading 31
    Employee Monitoring 31
Business Organization and Ethics 34
Business Regulations & Entities 35
    Market Competition and Monopolies 37
    Title VII 39
    Affirmative Action 40
    Comparable Worth 40
    ADA 41
    OSHA 41
    EPA 41
    FDA 42
    SA8000 42
Employee Relations 43
Minimum Wage 44
    WARN Act 45
    Confidentiality 45
    Whistle Blowing 46
    Sexual Harassment 48
    Discrimination 49

| Unions and Labor Relations 52
| Employee Polygraph Protection Act - EPPA 53
Corporations and Stakeholders 54
| Leadership Styles 59
| Codes of Ethics 60
Ethics in International Business 62
| International Organizations 62
| Cultural Ethics 63
| Multinational/Transnational Corporations 66
| Bribe or Grease Payment? 67
| Cultural Discrimination 68
| Outsourcing 69
| Insourcing 71
Ecology and Global Business 71
| Water Pollution 72
| Air Pollution 73
| Primary & Secondary Pollutants 74
| Environmental Regulations 74
| Sustainable Development 76
Business and Government 80
| Government Imposed Quality Standards 81
| Government Intervention 81
| Business and Politics 85
Sample Test Questions 88
Test Taking Strategies 144
What Your Score Means 144
Test Preparation 145
Legal Note 146

Business Ethics

Although there may once have been a day when a simple handshake could be considered to ensure a business transaction, business today requires far more monitoring and regulating. The study of business ethics is an attempt to apply moral principles to business operations. Ethics is closely associated with the term morality. Often the two terms are interchangeable, however there is a distinction. Morality is used to describe a person's character. It encompasses their beliefs about behaviors and can dictate how they act or respond in different situations. With morality, the focus tends to be on individuals. Ethics is the study of morality. It focuses on societal acceptance of and adherence to moral principles. Ethics focuses on the social structures which morals are a part of. Ethical principles can be considered generally accepted guidelines or expectations about the way that people (or businesses) behave.

There are three major categories of ethics, all of which come into play in the everyday operations of businesses. Three different schools of ethics are social ethics, economical ethics and legal ethics. Social ethics have to do with the way people interact with one another. For example, the morality of lying to or stealing from another person falls under social ethics. Economic ethics have to do with business and money related issues. For example, whether or not an American company with overseas offices or factories should have to abide by United States labor laws would fall under economic ethics.

Legal ethics has to do with the actions of lawyers. Things such as lawyer-client privilege fall under legal ethics. For example, one aspect of legal ethics is noisy withdrawals. A noisy withdrawal is when a lawyer becomes aware of frauds committed by their client and withdraws legal representation for their client. They then notify the proper authorities of what they know. For example, in cases involving the SEC, if a lawyer becomes aware of fraud or illegal activities by their client they should remove themselves and notify the SEC of the wrongdoing.

However, determining ethical principles that businesses should follow is not necessarily as straightforward as it sounds. This is because businesses thrive on the ability to generate a profit. Consider, for example, a grocery store. The store purchases the groceries from a supplier. In order to make a profit the grocery store must sell the groceries for more than they paid for them. At face value this may seem "wrong" of the company to do, they are knowingly overcharging all of their customers.

However, if they didn't then there would be no grocery stores and people would have to purchase groceries from the suppliers themselves – a much more difficult process in the end. Therefore, the perceived overcharging which could be considered unethical, truly benefits everyone involved. Of course, this is a simplified example, and not all business practices can be considered in these terms, nor do they have eventual benefits, but it serves to illustrate the point that ethics is not always a cut and dry situation. What it comes down to is that business ethics is a study of the extent to which an action can be viewed as necessary for businesses to thrive, and when it becomes entirely unethical.

For example, many scandals in the early 2000s served to increase the number of federal regulations involving business, and lowered people's trust in the business community as a whole. These scandals included well known people and companies, including Enron, Tyco International, Martha Stewart, Nike and Worldcom.

Enron was created in 1985 by the merging of two large gas pipeline companies. By 2000 it had become one of the largest companies in the United States, generating over $100 billion in revenues. Not surprisingly it came as a shock when just a year later (In 2001) the company declared bankruptcy, costing shareholders and investors billions. Under further investigation it was shown that the company had been using accounting practices that were not accurate and showed the company's financial situation in better light than it was by hiding its debt. This was done by creating legal entities called special-purpose entities (SPEs) and then having them assume the debt. This created the impression that Enron had more assets than it did, and that there was a healthy cash flow because the SPEs did not appear on the balance sheet.

Another company associated with accounting scandal is Tyco International. By the end of 2000, Tyco International was a major company, bringing in around 30 billion dollars. The company had three main divisions, involving fire protection, electronics and packaging. When Dennis Kozlowski became the company's Chief Executive Officer (CEO) in the early 1990s he proceeded to expand the business into other industries, and the company soon became one of the largest producers of medical equipment as well.

However, when the SEC launched an investigation of the company, it was discovered that Kozlowski had stolen millions from the company. As one example, he had purchased nearly 20 million dollars of art for himself and used company funds to pay for the art, and the taxes on it. He also threw an extravagant party for his wife using company funds. In total, it was determined that he had stolen around 75 million dollars. In addition, Kozlowski along with the company's Chief Financial Officer, Mark Schwartz, had arranged to have 7.5 million shares of stock (worth 450 billion dollars) sold without authorization, and then moved the money out of the company and into their own accounts. When the deceit came to light, Tyco International's stock prices dropped by 80%.

The scandals continued as another company, Worldcom, was forced to declare bankruptcy when an internal audit revealed billions of dollars of wrongly reported expenses. The company had been reporting operating expenses as investments. In total, the company had misreported over three billion dollars of expenses as investments. Correcting the financial statements showed that instead of growing, as it had appeared, the company was actually shrinking and in debt. Stock prices fell 99%, once again to the loss of shareholders in addition to over 15,000 people who lost their jobs.

These three incidents shook the securities markets as shareholders lost billions of dollars. The underhanded accounting practices of the three companies resulted in a widespread loss of confidence in the securities market. As a result of this loss of faith, the Sarbanes-Oxley Act was passed in 2002. The Sarbanes-Oxley Act tightened laws enforcing accounting and auditing practices with the intent of restoring stakeholder confidence in securities markets.

Another scandal involved Martha Stewart. Stewart built her company from a small gourmet food shop and catering business to founding Martha Stewart Living Omnimedia in 1996. She had become the iconic symbol of a homemaker and the company soon owned multiple magazines, TV programs, books and a newspaper and radio column. However, in 2001 she came under investigation for insider trading. Insider trading occurs when a person trades stock when they have information not available to the general public which influences their actions.

In Martha Stewart's case, the stock in question was ImClone stock, a pharmaceutical company for which her friend, Sam Waksal, was an executive. The day before ImClone's stock value plummeted because it was not given FDA approval for a new drug, Stewart sold off nearly a quarter million dollars of shares, along with Waksal, who sold off nearly five million dollars of shares. Both were eventually convicted of insider trading and Stewart was sentenced to five months in prison and five months under home arrest for her involvement. Insider trading, along with accounting practices, is an aspect considered under business ethics.

The Nike scandal started when it was discovered that the famous athletics brand was producing many of their products in Asian factories with low wages and dangerous working conditions that would not be acceptable in the United States. The company was soon barraged with complaints, and protests were held outside of many of their stores. Within two years their revenue and stock prices had been cut in half. As a result, the company began an exhaustive public relations campaign. They accepted responsibility for the working conditions in foreign factories, and began to work with the factory owners to improve them. They established work codes, and outlined steps to achieving them. In addition, the company went around the country to different universities to restore their image in the eyes of college students.

This scandal raises many questions about business ethics. For example, should United States based companies have to adhere to United States laws even when operating in foreign countries? Also, if so, should this be universally true – or extend only to certain laws? How should child labor, safety codes and wages be addressed? Should the United

States based company be held responsible for factory conditions, even if they do not own the factory that supplies their products (as was the case with Nike)? The list goes on, and all of the questions are ones that business ethics seeks to address. However, in many cases there is still not a satisfactory compromise.

Despite the many scandals of the past few decades, the evidence that better ethics actual helps businesses has become increasingly accepted. For example, some of the benefits of doing business ethically are that employees have an increased feeling of loyalty to the company. When employees feel that their company is essentially "good" they are more likely to want to continue working there. A track record of good ethics also increases loyalty from investors. If a company is doing reasonably well, and the investors feel that they can trust the company to be ethical in their practices, they feel more secure in investing in the company.

On the other hand, unethical practices (as shown through the examples above) typically result in downfall of stock prices and loss of profit for the company. By extension, good ethics is therefore healthy for a company's profit. When given the choice between an ethical company and an unethical company, people are more likely to purchase from a company they consider ethical. Consider the example of Nike. Their revenues fell by 50% and people were protesting in front of their stores when they felt like the company was being unethical. Practicing good business ethics has become a way for companies to give themselves a competitive advantage over other companies in their respective industries.

On the large scale, business ethics is also important, but not all ethical problems in business occur between one business and another business or between business and the public as a whole. Some ethical issues apply to the proceedings within business, and these issues also come under the scrutiny of business ethics. For example, issues of conflict of interest, sexual harassment, nondisclosure agreements and discrimination are all addressed by the field of business ethics as well.

 Moral Philosophies & Business Ethics

FUNDAMENTALS OF ETHICS

In order to form a basis from which to determine whether or not something is unethical, it must first be determined what the criteria are for something to be considered ethical. The fundamentals of ethics have been discussed and debated for thousands of years, and there are many different schools of thought which can be ascribed to. Consider, for example, if a person is judged on the consequence of their action. Does that mean that a good intentioned person whose actions accidentally result in a negative situation was acting immorally? Conversely, what if a person had bad intentions and inadvertently brought about a positive result. Does this mean that they were truly acting morally? Think instead, of if people are judged based on the morality of the actions themselves instead of on the consequence of their actions. What does this mean about a person who steals food to keep their family from starving?

Going further, what are the criteria for labeling an action or outcome as good or bad? Hedonism is one theory which claims that a person's happiness or pleasure is the only ultimate good. In essence, if something makes a person happy, it must have been a moral action. This view is contrasted by pluralists (also called nonhedonists) who believe that good is the result of many factors, and that no single action can be labeled as good. Elements which pluralists consider as measures of good are personal health, intelligence, art and personal happiness.

Even in terms of business it can be difficult to determine what is moral, immoral, good or bad. It might seem that a business's wealth or economic success could be considered a good outcome. However, there are boundaries to what a business is allowed to do to further their own position. When highly successful companies are discovered to have participated in acts that the public considers unethical it can be absolutely devastating to the company. They lose revenue and the goodwill of the public. Consider Enron for example. It could be argued that they were merely acting hedonistically and in everyone's best interest – by hiding the company's debt they were keeping stock prices high which brought money to the company, its owners and its shareholders. Therefore, they were bringing happiness to a large number of people. Yet their actions were unmistakably unethical. Clearly there is no single theory which is considered more correct any other theory. There are merely many ways of looking at situations, and many opinions about what makes an action good or bad.

The nature of what is good gives rise to, in a general sense, two different types of perspectives. These are egoism and relativism. **Egoism** is the belief that people should act only in their best interests. In other words, if it benefits the person it is the right thing for them to do. One problem with this theory, however, is that there is really no way to determine what is in the person's best interest. Should it, for example, be considered in the short term in which case many acts that would normally be seen as unethical – such as cheating, lying or stealing – could be justified, or should it be considered in the long term in which case these acts would likely prove to the eventual detriment of the individual. Another problem that arises in a business sense, is that often there are contrasting issues. For example, when the executives of Tyco International were stealing money from the company, there was an initially a benefit to them- they could live extravagant, wealthy lifestyles. However, the long term resulted in their downfalls. They spent time in prison, lost their jobs and owed the company money.

Relativism is the theory that ethics is subject to society. In other words, there really is no universal set of morals because they are determined by the state and opinion of the society in which one lives. One problem with this theory, however, is that there are some issues for which there is not necessarily a widely accepted moral opinion. Also, the theory implies that a person must follow societal norms to be acting ethically.

For example, in the United States there is a federally imposed minimum wage which is higher than in other countries. According to relativist theory it would be unethical for a business to not pay their employees minimum wage. However, if that business had branches in other countries where there was either no minimum wage or a lower minimum wage, then it is no longer unethical for the company to not adhere to the standard. This seems counterintuitive because it is the same company, however according to relativist theory the goodness of the action is determined by society and the company should feel no obligation to pay their foreign employees well.

In the case of both relativism and egoism there are cases in which the definition of goodness can be applied, however it seems that neither creates an entirely satisfactory, all-inclusive definition of what is good or bad. This is one of the challenges of ethics.

KOHLBERG'S MODEL OF COGNITIVE MORAL DEVELOPMENT

Lawrence Kohlberg, a psychologist, developed a theory which outlined six stages which he believed that people went through as their mental and moral understanding developed. This theory is called Kohlberg's Model of Cognitive Moral Development. Kohlberg used the theories of Jean Piaget as a basis for his model Piaget studied the way that children learned as they got older. Kohlberg extended Piaget's model to apply to moral behaviors as well. He believed that all people progressed through the stages, one at a time in order (no stages could be skipped). Kohlberg's model looks at the motivations behind a person or businesses actions.

In stage one of Kohlberg's Model of Cognitive Moral Development a person is motivated by avoidance of punishment. Kohlberg believed this to be the most immature reason to do something. For example, a child does their chores to avoid being grounded. Their understanding is that doing their chores is the right thing to do because it saves them from punishment. This doesn't just apply to children however. Another example of motivation in the first stage is people who don't speed because they do not want to get a ticket. The behavior – driving slower then they prefer – is brought on by a want to avoid the punishment of the ticket. The reasoning, therefore, is that driving the speed limit must be the right thing to do because it helps to avoid the punishment of a ticket.

In the sphere of business the first stage describes a business which acts appropriately in an attempt to avoid the negative ramifications of breaking the law. For example, a company would prefer to pay their workers less than minimum wage, however if they were to do so their employees would most likely sue them for the difference in wages. Therefore, companies who require workers that are relatively unskilled, or easily replaceable, would typically follow a stage one mentality in paying their workers.

In stage two a person is motivated through seeking rewards. This isn't to say that they don't ever think about the punishments that may come as a result of their actions, but the primary reason that they make the choices that they do is because they know that they will benefit from it. For example, instead of a person driving slowly because they are afraid of getting a ticket, a person in stage two of Kohlberg's model would chose to not speed because they want the lower rates of car insurance that will result from not having any tickets.

In business terms this stage could be used to describe, for example, companies that donate large amounts of money to charity only because it is a tax write off. This is not to say that what they are doing is in some way wrong, just that their primary motivation is seeking benefits. The reasoning being, therefore, that donating money is the right thing to do because it has a positive consequence for the business.

Another example is companies that require highly specialized and skilled workers. Skilled workers get paid more than unskilled workers (such as in the stage one example) because they are less easily replaceable. Therefore, companies will offer such workers more and more money so that they will chose to work for them instead of another company. This behavior isn't brought on by an effort to be generous to the worker or to make their lives better and more fulfilling. Rather, the behavior is induced by the company's need for the worker, and therefore it is a stage two mentality. The company is paying the worker more because it benefits them in the end.

In stage three a person is motivated by how they believe their actions will be perceived, and also by how it benefits or hurts other people. In this stage a person considers whether their action will gain them approval from others or heighten their status in other's eyes. For example, instead of a person not wanting to get a speeding ticket because it would heighten their insurance premiums, an individual in stage three would not want to get a speeding ticket because of what their friends and family would think of them if they did. At this level, the person would consider what they did to be wrong or immoral because it lowered their peer's opinion of them.

Businesses that deal with nuclear waste, for example, must be very careful of how they deal with that waste so that people will not develop a negative opinion of them. A negative public opinion could make it harder for the company to get approval for their business operations. Obviously it would be cheaper for companies to just dump the waste somewhere, but that would be dangerous to the surrounding areas. If a company chooses to dispose of their nuclear waste properly only because they worry about the negative opinions that customers would have if they did not (and not because they had any particular care for the negative impacts to the people or environment), they would be in stage three. By their reasoning, disposing of nuclear waste improperly is wrong because it generates negative opinions about the company.

Another example would be if an assistant manager was told by the manager of a factory that the output was not great enough, and that the machines needed to start running faster, forcing the workers to produce more products quickly. The assistant manager (if his reasoning followed the stage three level of cognitive moral development) would consider not only the consequences for himself if he did or did not obey the order, but whether the increased production would benefit the workers and if it would make them happier (such as if it increased their wages) or if it would merely make them angry with him.

In stage four, a person is motivated by the demands of authority figures. People in this stage will feel that something is right because they are told to do it by a person in charge (or that it is wrong because they are told not to do it). Stage four naturally leads to people following the laws because they believe that it is inherently right to follow the laws and inherently wrong to break them. For example, a person would want to avoid getting a speeding ticket not because they cared in any way about the consequences, but because they just feel that it is wrong to speed.

This stage describes a business which just follows the laws. For example, instead of the company from the stage three example disposing of their nuclear waste properly because they worry about public opinion of them, from a stage four standpoint the company would dispose of the nuclear waste properly because it is the law to do so.

An assistant manager who was told by the manager of a factory to increase production would, from a stage four standpoint, do so without really questioning it. This illustrates the main difference between stage three and stage for of Kohlberg's Model of Cognitive Moral Development. Although in both stages morality is derived from sources other than the person directly, in stage three the focus is on more of a collective opinion and in stage four the focus is on authority figures.

In stage five a person is motivated by an obligation to society. They recognize that other people have their own opinions and viewpoints, and are concerned with the affect that their actions have on society. The person works to achieve happiness for all, and learns to compromise. In this stage particularly, the idea of a social contract (a balancing between rights and responsibilities held by individuals that is to the benefit of all people) becomes relevant. For example, in stage five a person would choose not to speed because they feel that it is their obligation to drive safely. They don't want to be responsible for an accident which could harm another person.

Returning to the nuclear waste example, the company would choose to dispose of their nuclear waste properly, not because of any outside source's opinion, but because they felt obligated to society to ensure that no one was harmed by the nuclear waste that they had generated. The company would consider it to be their responsibility to act for the safety of society and the environment.

In stage six a person believes in adherence to universal ethical principles. A person's actions are taken out of a personal feeling and opinion of morality and correctness. This stage is characterized by people being ruled by their consciences. Kohlberg believed that few people, if any, achieved this degree of moral development.

Kohlberg's six stages are often broken down into three, more general, levels. The first level is called pre-conventional morality. This level encompasses the first two stages. Therefore, decisions in this stage are made through simple understanding of punishment and reward systems. The person is concerned with their immediate interests. The second level is called conventional morality.

This level encompasses stages three and four. In this stage a person's main focus is on fitting societal norms and meeting expectations. The final level is post conventional. In the post conventional stage a person is ruled by conscience instead of society. This breakdown illustrates that as a person moves through the six stages, their moral development advances from a morality determined through self-interest, to one determined by society, to one determined by the individual.

CONSEQUENTIALISM

Moving on to actual morality theories, one of the most basic terms associated with moral theories is consequentialism. Consequentialism is a broad term which refers to any type of moral theory which determines the morality of an action based upon the result or consequence that it produces. For example, a business donates money to their local food bank. This money is used to provide food to homeless families who would otherwise have starved. According to consequentialism, this was a moral act. However, by the same theory, if a person steals food from a grocery store it would also be considered moral because it has the same positive consequence of feeding people.

The most straightforward type of consequentialism is called teleological ethics. Often teleology is used interchangeably with consequentialism. **Teleological ethics** claims that if the consequence of the action is good then the action is considered moral. If the consequence of the action is bad then the action is considered immoral. Different types of teleological ethics consider how to determine whether the consequence of the action should be considered good or bad.

For example, egoism (which was described above) is considered a form of teleological ethics. This is because egoism considers the "goodness" of an action based on the consequences that it has for the individual.

MILL'S UTILITARIANISM

John Stuart Mill is known for developing a teleological theory called utilitarianism. **Utilitarianism** is a social theory which attributes an action's morality to its positive and negative consequences. It operates based on what came to be known as the greatest-happiness principle. This principle can be described as "the greatest good for the greatest number of people." This means that the good that comes about because of an action must outweigh the bad that comes about for it to be a moral action. This mindset essentially involves doing a cost benefit analysis for each situation that arises. If the benefits exceed the costs (i.e., if it causes more good than harm) then the action is moral. Otherwise the action is immoral.

For example, considering the Tyco International scandal, a utilitarian would first look at the benefits that came about because of the executives' dishonesty. Their lives were arguably enriched because of the excess funds. Then, a utilitarian would consider the negative aspects of the executives' dishonesty. The company lost revenue, the scandal caused a drop in stock prices that cost investor's money, employees lost their jobs and the executives spent time in jail. Weighting the positives and negatives against one another the most sensible determination is that the executives were acting unethically.

Mill also believed that there were different levels of happiness, and that some ranked above others. According to Mill, intellectual and moral pleasure is of greater value than contentment or physical pleasure. In essence, a large amount of pleasure from simple pleasures is not preferable to even a small amount of pleasure from an intellectual venue. For example, a college student has the choice between going to a movie with friends – which would benefit their social life and allow them to relax and have fun – and going to their classes – which would benefit them in the future by helping them understand the class better, get better grades and eventually get a better job. According to Mill, with all else being equal it is more morally correct for the student to go to class because of the intellectual benefit, as opposed to the movie.

It may seem obvious in this case that the more intellectual option is the better to choose, however the choice isn't always so simply. Consider, for example, a pharmaceutical company. Understandably, the greatest portion of the company's revenues are going to be made in more highly developed countries in which the citizens have more disposable income (income which they can spend how they choose). Because of this the company's research are marketing are both going to be geared toward products that will increase their revenue from these sources, such as diet medications or cosmetic treatments. If the companies were not to focus on developing these products, they would not be able to generate enough income to stay in business. However, in the meantime, in lesser developed regions of the world such as Africa there are thousands of people a day dying from illnesses such as AIDS, Malaria and various tropical diseases. The problem is that the price of the life-saving drugs, even when offered at production prices, is greater than the average person can afford to pay. Considered from Mill's utilitarian standpoint, the pharmaceutical companies are acting unethically because they are focusing on the less valued happiness of cosmetic, or physical, pleasures, instead of on the more important intellectual and moral happiness that would result from the development of life saving medications.

Since Mill developed this theory, it is has evolved to include two different ways of approaching utilitarianism. These ways are called act utilitarianism and rule utilitarianism.

ACT AND RULE UTILITARIANISM

The first of the two, act utilitarianism, consists of a person examining a situation, considering all the possible actions they could take and deciding which one would end most favorably for all involved. Act utilitarianism is so named because it considers the consequences of the specific action which a person is considered. It is a situation based method of determining ethics. Because act utilitarians consider actions in specific situational contexts, general rules of conduct hold little significance for them except as possible general guidelines. For example, when told that "killing is wrong" an act utilitarian would likely agree not because they find anything inherently wrong with killing, but because killing people is detrimental to society as a whole. When given a specific situation, such as self-defense, killing becomes ethical.

For example, consider a business that is based in the United States, but is considering building a factory in India and outsourcing the production of their products in an effort to increase revenue. When the company is setting up their new factory, they will have to hire employees to operate the machines. For the company's locations in the United States, they pay their workers just above the federally mandated minimum wage. They consider this to be an ethical practice because if they didn't the negative repercussions to their business would be tremendous. They would likely face lawsuits, would have a hard time finding workers and their customers would have a low opinion of them. However, in expanding to India the company realizes that the minimum wage in India is only about a third of the minimum wage in the United States. Therefore, the company offers its employees just over a third of what they pay their workers in the United States. From an act utilitarian standpoint, the company is entirely ethical in both situations. Because they consider the two situations independently of one another, the company does not have to treat all of their workers the same to be justified.

The second type of utilitarianism, **rule utilitarianism**, consists of a person considering an action independently of a situation and determining whether or not it is moral as a general rule. The rule utilitarian determines the morality of these rules based on the extent to which they result in the greatest good for society. Basically they consider the results (or consequences) of different situations to determine which is the most acceptable. This type of reasoning does not allow for exceptions under different circumstances as does act utilitarianism. In contrast to act utilitarianism, where general rules hold little significance, rule utilitarianism is entirely defined by sets of general rules. For example, if a rule utilitarian believes that "killing is wrong," then even in situations where killing would be considered self-defense, it would not be considered ethical. However, this is not to say that rule utilitarians just blanketly accept rules that are dictated by the morality of society. If a rule utilitarian is told that "lying is wrong," but after considering the rule themselves they decide, for some reason, that lying is more beneficial to society than telling the truth, they will advocate a change in the rule.

Consider now a company which follows a rule utilitarian pattern of ethics which is in the same situation as the company which follows an act utilitarian pattern of ethics. They have come to a similar conclusion about pay as the act utilitarian company, and believe that "it is not ethical to pay workers less than nine dollars an hour" for many of the same reasons that the act utilitarian company paid their workers just above minimum wage. However, when the rule utilitarian company expands to foreign countries, they would either have to reevaluate their rule, or pay all of their employees, no matter what country they are in, the same amount to be acting ethically. Of course, if the company's rule was that "it is not ethical to pay workers less than minimum wage" then they could lower the pay for employees in countries with a low minimum wage.

Thus far, all of the different theories discussed have been consequential, or based upon consequences. There are also many moral theories which fall under the category of nonconsequential ethics. These types of ethical theories do not believe that the consequence of an action is the most important factor in determining its morality, as in consequentialism, but rather consider certain actions to be inherently moral, and others to be inherently immoral.

DEONTOLOGY

One type of nonconsequential ethics is deontology. **Deontological ethics** is based around the idea of duty ("deon" derives from the Greek for duty). In contrast to utilitarianism, in deontology it would be considered immoral for a person to harm another even if it resulted in a greater benefit to society. Deontologists claim that there are things that regardless of consequence a person should or should not do. Deontologists consider the rights of the individuals involved as well as the intentions of an action in determining its morality. For example, if a worker in a company which produced radioactive materials were exposed to the radiation due to poor safety practices by the company, a deontological minded company would feel obligated to increase safety measures at any cost, even bankruptcy. In contrast, a utilitarian company would consider whether the life of the employee was worth the financial stability of the company.

KANTIAN ETHICS

One type of the most well-known types of deontological theory is Kantian ethics. The philosophy of Kantian ethics was developed by Immanuel Kant. Kant believed that the sole indicator of morality was the person's motivation for performing an action. The question that follows is what makes a motive good or bad. Many of the moral theories that have been discussed so far equate a moral act with its ability to generate happiness - either for the person performing the act or for others or for society as a whole. However, Kant completely separated morality and happiness. He believed that happiness was more a result of luck than it was a result of any choices that a person could make. He believed that to be considered good, a motive would need to be both unconditional and universal. For example, say that a person is motivated to steal from a store because they are hungry. Their motivation cannot be universalized. If every person were to act the same way as the person who stole, then the stores would have to close down because they would not be able to make a profit. Therefore, the motive is immoral.

According to Kant, there is only one truly good motive – good will, which Kant defines as acting out of a sense of duty. Because good will is the only good motive, the only actions that are moral are those which are performed out of a sense of duty, or feeling that it is the "right" thing to do. For example, donating money to a charity because you feel bad for the people it supports would not be moral. However, donating money because you feel that it is what you should do is moral.

Kant is most famous for his development of what is called the categorical imperative. Essentially the categorical imperative is just a method for testing a set of maxims by which people should live. Kant believed that people should create sets of maxims, or rules which dictate their actions, through which they consider all their actions and choices. The categorical imperative consists of two "tests." These two tests are just the conditions which were described above - a maxim must be unconditional and universal.

That a maxim must be unconditional means that it cannot be self-contradictory nor have exceptions. To carry out this test the maxim must be generalized. For example, if a person decides to enter into a contract, with no intention of fulfilling their end of the deal, the generalization would be that all people can enter into contracts with no intention of fulfilling their ends of the deals. This maxim would therefore not pass the unconditional test because it is self-contradictory. If everyone entered into a contract and didn't fulfill their end of the deal then no one would enter into contracts because they would hold no meaning.

Another example which fails the unconditional test would be false advertising. If a company advertises a product in a purposefully misleading way, the generalization would be that all companies should engage in false advertising. However, if no companies were advertising truthfully then people would not pay any heed to advertising and the purpose would be defeated. Therefore, under Kantian ethics false advertising is immoral because it is not unconditional. In the case of false advertising there are actually federal laws which prevent companies from being unethical. The Federal Trade Commission Act was passed in 1914 and, in addition to creating the Federal Trade Commission, it dictated that advertising cannot be deceptive or unfair, and it must be backed up by evidence. This policy of honest advertising is referred to as truth in advertising.

The second condition – that a maxim must be universal – basically means that if you applied the principle universally it has to create conditions that a person would be willing to live under (or that a person would choose to live under). This rule comes into play for maxims that may be unconditional, but would be detrimental to society if they were considered acceptable on a wide scale. For example, a person may say that they will not help anyone who does not have the ability to compensate them, even though the cost to themselves would be minimal. The generalization would be that no person would help another who does not have the ability to compensate them, even at minimal costs to themselves. It is feasible that the world could operate under these conditions; therefore, the maxim passes the test of being unconditional. However, if the maxim were universalized it would create a world where people do not donate to charity or do not help a person who is stranded on the side of the road. Also, if people only helped people that could compensate them, it would create a world where people would not call the fire station when their neighbor's house was on fire - it does not directly benefit them to help their neighbor. Most likely a person would not chose to live in a world like this, and therefore the maxim does not pass the second test.

Kant described maxims, or **categorical imperatives**, as distinct from what he called hypothetical imperatives. While maxims are universal, hypothetical imperatives are more situation specific. Hypothetical imperatives are essentially instructions on how to either achieve or not achieve a goal. Usually they are in the form of if-then statements. For example, if a person's goal was that they wanted to do well on an exam, a hypothetical imperative that they may follow would be "if I want to do well on the exam then I should study."

Alternatively, if a person's goal were to not get arrested, their hypothetical imperative may be "if I do not want to get arrested, then I should not break the law." Kant did not believe that hypothetical imperatives could be used to measure morality. This is because they are, by definition, attached to a goal. Under Kantian ethics, the morality of an action is not judged based on the result of the action. In addition, if the hypothetical imperative did not apply to a person, such as if they didn't really care if they passed the exam or got arrested, then they would simply ignore it. For this reason Kant asserts that the categorical imperative version (such as "don't break the law") is a better judgment of morality than the hypothetical imperatives.

Another type of imperative which has become a part of Kantian ethics is called the practical imperative. The practical imperative simply states that people are to treat humanity as an end and never as a means. The practical imperative is really just a specific categorical imperative. It is designed to prevent exploitation. If a person considers the betterment of humanity as the acceptable result of a maxim, then they will not adopt any maxims which are detrimental to humanity as a whole.

For example, the **Truth in Lending Act (TILA)** is one regulation which prevents lenders from exploiting those that they lend money to (and by extension from violating the practical imperative). The Act requires that certain information be disclosed when a person is applying for a loan or credit card so that they can more easily compare different options. For example, TILA requires that things like the finance charge, schedule of payments and annual percentage rates (APR) are disclosed. It also requires that it is disclosed when a credit card has a yearly or monthly fee attached to it. This prevents consumers from exploitation which arises from a lack of information about their transactions.

VIRTUE ETHICS

An additional ethical theory to consider is virtue ethics. The theory of virtue ethics is that as people develop and interact with one another they acquire a certain moral character. They decide which things they think are moral and immoral. People will then act according to what they believe is moral. They will be honest if they find honesty moral, and they will be kind if they find kindness moral.

COMPARING ETHICAL PERSPECTIVES

Because of all of the different ways to consider ethics, people given the same situation can often chose different courses of action, and for many different reasons. Consider, for example, a salesperson who distributes tasers to policemen across the country. Assume that the salesperson knows that the tasers in a particular batch have been manufactured incorrectly and have a 2% chance of backfiring on the user. The FBI has just ordered a new shipment and the salesperson must decide whether they should inform the FBI about the defect, or ignore it and sell the tasers anyway.

If the salesperson considers the situation from an egoist standpoint, he will consider the consequences to himself if he informs the FBI or doesn't. He would most likely consider the fact that if he informed the FBI about the defect, he would most likely lose the sale. His income would decrease and his reputation would be ruined. However, if he chooses not to inform the FBI the chances of an officer's taser misfiring is fairly low, and they may never even have a problem. Even if they did, the consequence to the salesperson would be minimal – it would probably get written off as a random accident. Therefore, the salesperson would most likely not inform the FBI about the defect and would continue with the sale.

If the salesperson considered the situation from a rule utilitarian standpoint, they would consider whether it were ethical as a general rule to sell defective products. They would consider all of the outcomes in situations where defective products were sold. Most likely, they would determine that as a general rule, it would be unethical to sell defective products, and therefore would inform the FBI of the defect.

If the salesperson considered the situation from an act utilitarian standpoint, they would consider the outcome for all involved. The salesperson knows that if they go through with the sale, it is possible that the defect puts a policeman's life in danger if the taser misfires. However, they would consider that the chance of a misfire was remote. Also, if they inform the FBI of the defect and the FBI cancels their order, they would have to use time and resources to find another vendor, and the policemen would be entirely without tasers until they could do so. Therefore, knowing the benefit and costs to both themselves and the FBI, the person may choose to continue with the sale because it is more favorable for them and the FBI to just get through with the sale.

If the salesperson considered the situation from a Kantian standpoint, they would generalize the situation into a maxim. For example, "I will sell defective products." To test the maxim they would consider whether it is unconditional. If everyone sold defective products, then no one would want to buy products from other people, so the maxim is not unconditional. Therefore, the salesperson would determine that it would be unethical to continue with the sale, and inform the FBI of the defect.

It is also important to consider, along with different moral theories, the way that these theories can influence decision making in business. Often people adhere to different ethical and behavioral standards in their personal and professional lives. For example, people wait until they are acknowledged to talk, or in the case of school they raise their hand to talk, though they typically wouldn't do so in home situations.

 Social Responsibility

The term social responsibility is often used interchangeably with ethics, especially as it applies to businesses. Specifically, social responsibility reflects the expectations and standards which are embodied in a business based on the collective concerns of owners (this includes shareholders), employees, suppliers and the community that the business is in. Many people feel that businesses should consider and practice Corporate Social Responsibility (CSR). CSR is also called corporate citizenship.

CSR (or corporate citizenship) describes the consideration of large companies about the well-being of society when they make business decisions. CSR requires that companies consider people and the environment along with their own profit. The need for CSR is often debated. Some feel that mandating CSR disrupts the normal function of an economy and over-regulates business practices. Others believe that these concerns are outweighed by the negative impacts caused by irresponsible business practices. The debate cycles back to what people specifically believe are the responsibilities of a business.

In 1991, Archie Carroll wrote an article titled "The Pyramid of Corporate Social Responsibility." He focused and defined the corporate social responsibility pyramid.

There are four different levels of responsibility which can be taken into consideration. They are economic responsibilities, legal responsibilities, ethical responsibilities and philanthropic responsibilities. In some cases these responsibilities build on each other, and in other cases they may come into conflict. For example, a company which is fulfilling philanthropic responsibilities could also be said to be fulfilling ethical responsibilities. On the other hand, economic and legal responsibilities may conflict if the business could make more money as a result of engaging in illegal behaviors.

Economic responsibilities are generally considered the most basic and fundamental level of responsibility that a company can adhere to. The company's economic responsibilities refer to its attempts to maximize profits and do the best it can as a business financially. This type of responsibility is fairly obvious because generating profit or wealth for the owner's is nearly always the purpose of business. Of course, for non-profit organizations (such as a cancer charity) the generation of revenue is still important for the organization to fulfill its purpose although not the primary target.

As obvious as this level of ethics may seem, there are cases where people do not act in the best interest of their company. For example, consider the Tyco International scandal. CEO Dennis Kozlowski was literally stealing millions of dollars from the company, and his deceit eventually came back to cost shareholders billions of dollars.

Kozlowski failed at the most basic level of ethics – ensuring the greatest benefits to the shareholders.

For some people, this level is all that they believe should be required of businesses. However, it can become more complex as one considers what is involved in a company pursuing only economic benefits. Often, it is not feasible for a company to exclusively consider economic benefits. Most simply, the reason for this is that at some point a company pursuing purely economic benefits would encounter legal conflicts.

For example, imagine there were a situation in which committing an illegal act would increase a company's revenues (such as misleading advertising). However, if the act was discovered the company would be prosecuted which could result in the end of the business. Because of the number of regulations affecting business, legal responsibilities would invariably have to come into play for the business to continue operating.

Therefore, more common than the belief that a company should consider only economic benefits is the belief that a company should consider just economic and legal responsibilities. This sort of approach to a business's responsibilities would dictate that as long as a business is acting within the constraints of the law, the only concern of the management should be to maximize the economic benefits to the company. In this case, a company faced with possible monetary gains if a law is broken they would be socially responsible to follow the law. This choice to follow the law does not necessarily stem from a moral objection to breaking the law, just the expectation that the business will abide by that level of responsibility.

The legal responsibilities of a business, or its responsibility to know and abide by government regulations, can come into play in multiple levels of the business. Regulations can cover everything from employee issues such as privacy and wages, to issues of international trade. Business regulations change often. Generally these changes will come about because of the opinion of the general population about current business practices. For example, if lots of people are angry about the fact that price of a product, say flour, is rising at higher rates than usual, then a politician may campaign with a platform of instituting a price ceiling (or legal limit) on the price of flour.

Economic and legal responsibilities can be considered the "must do" things of a business. If a business doesn't consider its economic responsibilities, the chances are that the business will fail. Therefore, the business must consider its economic responsibilities. Also, as was mentioned earlier, if a business doesn't consider its legal responsibilities the chances are that it will get shut down for either inadvertently or purposefully breaking a law. These are the most fundamental responsibilities that businesses have. Where most of the debate about CSR comes into play is in considering the other possible responsibilities. Specifically, whether ethical and philanthropic responsibilities are also "must do" aspects of a business, or whether they fall into a category of "can do" aspects.

The ethical responsibilities of a business can be considered as whether they follow acceptable standards of behavior. This is considered primarily in terms of the stakeholder's opinions and standards. The term ethical culture refers to the extent to which the company works to ensure that certain ethical standards are met. The idea of creating a corporate ethical culture is to minimize the need within the business for specific regulations.

The recent trend is that business is moving away from legally based regulations and toward creating an ethical culture that will make ethical behaviors a standard part of the business. Even on the international level organizations such as NAFTA and the WTO are working to develop universalized ethical standards. Although to a large extent the ethical responsibilities of a business are not mandated, more and more businesses are beginning to recognize that there are in fact benefits that come from increasing the ethical practices within a business.

One way that businesses benefit from ethical practices is through employee commitment. When a company is willing to consider the needs of their employees, the employees will feel more loyal to the company. Creating an ethical culture within a workplace also increases the ability of different individuals to work together which increases productivity.

Another way that businesses can benefit from ethical practices is that it contributes to investor loyalty. A person that believes that the company is "good" is more likely to invest in it than a person who is considering investments purely in terms of monetary compensation. Also, when a company is believed to have a strong ethical culture people will be more trusting of financial statements and more likely to give the company the benefit of the doubt. Considering the number of ethical scandals in the past decade, investors will be more wary of companies believed to have a more shaky ethical culture.

A third way that businesses can benefit from a strong ethical culture is that it contributes to customer satisfaction. Many businesses have found that one of the best economic strategies is ensuring repeat customers. From an advertising and marketing standpoint there is a much greater cost in finding new customers than in focusing on past customers. If a customer believes that a business is unethical, they are less likely to return.

Additionally, there are many examples of times when customers "boycotted" or refused to buy products because they disagreed with the product or company from an ethical standpoint. Nike sales fell when they were accused of supporting child labor and sweatshop conditions in their overseas factories. Many tuna companies faced reduced sales when it was discovered that their nets also resulted in the death of dolphins. Even going back to the earlier history of the United States, the British colonists refused to buy tea from the East India Company because they disagreed fundamentally with the tax imposed on it. Clearly customer satisfaction and opinions of an ethical nature can have a large influence on the success of the business.

The final type of responsibilities, philanthropic responsibilities, can also be important to the success of the business. Philanthropic responsibilities refer to the ways that the company "gives back" to the communities in which it operates. Although to a small extent ethical responsibilities are required in the form of regulations restricting unethical practices, philanthropic responsibilities are essentially entirely unregulated. Because philanthropic responsibilities are essentially charitable acts, it is fundamentally impossible for there to be any sort of requirements or regulations surrounding them.

The ideas of altruism and reciprocity are closely tied with a company's philanthropic responsibilities. Altruism refers to placing the good of another person above oneself. This is essentially what is being done when businesses engage in philanthropy. They are placing the good of those receiving the benefit of their acts above their own bottom line profit. Reciprocity is the idea that people should treat others in a way that reflects how they would like to be treated (the "golden rule"). Implied in this is that as businesses act altruistically it will come to benefit them in the long run.

The debate over corporate social responsibility really comes down to whether or not it should be considered a moral obligation of businesses to engage in philanthropy. For example, after Hurricane Katrina in 2005, Wal-Mart responded by setting up temporary stores through which to distribute free supplies, such as food, water or diapers, to those in need. They were also instrumental in helping government agencies coordinate logistics. Not all philanthropic works by a business have to be this large-scale. Philanthropy could describe a business donating food or supplies to a local food bank or homeless shelter. Other than donations, it is also considered philanthropy when a business creates awareness about a cause, or offers workshops or classes about issues of public concern.

Philanthropic actions help a business in developing its reputation. Ethics can play an important part in developing reputation, but philanthropy is what really cements the idea. A good reputation can take decades to develop, and then be lost as a result of one mistake. Even a business with a good reputation from decades of existence can for years after a negative incident find its every decision scrutinized and criticized by media, government agencies, investors, financial analysts and the regular consumer.

As shown with the benefits of practicing good ethics, a good reputation can really make the difference in the business world. It affects everyone from employees to investors to consumers. In a very real sense, a business's reputation can be what gives it its value. Consider major companies such as Wal-Mart, Coca-Cola or Microsoft. If a person or organization wanted to purchase one of these companies, they would have to pay billions of dollars (and rightly so). The reason for this is that the person wouldn't just be buying the physical company – its buildings, transportation equipment and inventory – they would have to pay for the reputation of the company. There are intangible benefits which come as a result of having a good reputation. (In accounting this amount in addition to the actual tangible assets that a company owns is referred to as a company's goodwill.)

As time progresses it becomes increasingly apparent that the attempt to maximize economic profits (and therefore fulfill economic responsibilities) for a company is largely interconnected with the ability to execute ethical and philanthropic responsibilities. This can be explained by understanding the terms shareholder and stakeholder. A shareholder is a person who literally owns a part of a corporation.

In other words, it is a person who has purchased stocks, or shares, of a company. Stakeholders are people who are affected by the decisions that the company makes. This can include not only the shareholders, but also the managers and other employees, people who reside in the area and customers of the company. Although stakeholders may not have a financial interest in the company, they do have the ability to affect its success. Therefore, it is essential that companies manage both shareholder and stakeholder interests in order to maximize the profits to the shareholders.

Boards of directors are responsible for hiring managers and important corporate officers. Therefore it is important that they are well acquainted with the needs of both shareholders and stakeholders. The ultimate responsibility for success or failure lies with their decisions. There have been times, for example, that shareholders were able to sue the board of directors after the failure of a company. The directors were left paying the large amounts of money out of their own resources.

Because the board of directors is so important in a corporation, there have been increasing demands for accountability and transparency from them. In the past, a member of a board of directors were often prior managers or executive officers of company, or friends of current directors or executives. However, recently the tendency has been to favor investors from outside the company, because their interest in the success of the firm is less biased or tainted by prior experience. Directors chosen from outside the company are also chosen based on their expertise and qualifications, meaning they are typically more capable.

The issue that tends to dominate a large portion of the board of directors' time is that of executive compensation (how much to pay company executives). In order to ensure that the executives have goals that are aligned with the best interests of the company, they are typically given bonuses based on performance and stock options so that they benefit personally from the success of the company (all on top of a base salary). Many people disapprove of the high benefits given to executives and the board of directors must consider how to balance that disapproval with the need to ensure that executives have a vested interest in the company and will not quickly abandon it if another company offers higher benefits.

If a company recognizes the importance of social responsibility, they will need to institute programs to ensure that it is being applied effectively. There are many ways to go about doing this, but a few of the possible steps would be to consider the corporate culture of the company, identify the various groups of stakeholders and their needs, tailor the company to best conform to their social responsibility commitments and gaining stakeholder feedback to ensure that the company is achieving its goals.

Although there are various opinions concerning the responsibilities of businesses, a policy in which companies consider all four types of responsibilities (economic, legal, ethical and philanthropic) is increasing in popularity as it proves to be a reliable way of maximizing the success of the company as a whole.

Ethics in Information

One of the most important factors in the business world is information. Businesses collect information about their operations, such as their employees, the cost of producing products or providing services, the differences in sales between different branches or the effectiveness of different market strategies in different areas. They collect information about the places in which they operate such as seasonal or cultural differences that will help them market better. They collect information about customers, and try determine, for example, which types of customers buy which types of products, the demographics of the areas in which they operate, financial information for their customers and other factors. Clearly information is one of the driving forces of effective business operations. With the massive amounts of information in circulation there are many opportunities for unethical behavior with respect to business. Various types of fraud are an example of unethical behaviors.

MARKETING

In a general sense, fraud is any deliberate attempt to deceive, manipulate or conceal facts. Marketing fraud, such as misleading advertisements, can also occur in many different ways. For example, in addition to refraining from employing misleading sales techniques, it is also important that businesses ensure that the content of their advertisements is not offensive. If a company creates an advertisement that many customers find offensive it would be detrimental to the company. It is beneficial to the company to be more conscientious about how their marketing practices are perceived by consumers in order to make them more effective. This way they can know if their advertisements are inadvertently creating a public opinion that the company is unethical.

One example that has previously been discussed is the idea of truth in advertising. These government mandated policies are ways that businesses are restricted from acting unethically in providing information to customers. In a business sense, advertising is an area in which there is a large temptation to be unethical. The whole point of advertising is to create a competitive advantage over customers that will make them more likely to come to the company which displayed the advertisements. Some types of misleading advertising include puffery, implied falsity and literal falsity.

Puffery is essentially exaggeration, or making claims that are not reasonable and mislead customers. Implied falsity occurs when an advertisement is technically true on a literal basis, but by nature has a tendency to mislead or confuse customers. Literal falsity, on the other hand, is not even technically true in its nature. By requiring that advertisements for companies maintain a sense of truthfulness and are not misleading, the companies are required to provide more accurate information. Participating in any of these actions would be considered fraud.

All of these examples of marketing fraud have to do with how products are promoted. There are many ways that companies can use advertising unethically. These ways can be considered by how they fit into the four P's of advertising. They are product, place, promotion and price. With each of these four P's there is an opportunity for companies to act unethically, such as through untruthful promotions (a problem which is regulated through truth in advertising laws).

PRICING STRATEGIES

There are also ways in which unethical marketing can be practiced outside of types of promotions, such as through different pricing strategies. Something is considered unethical if it is meant to be deceptive, convince buyers that they are getting more value for their many than they are or neglecting to provide accurate information about the conditions of the sale (which would also relate to truth in lending). For example, often times there will be a recommended price printed on an object that is being sold. If a company has recommended prices on the products that purposefully higher than they intend to sell them at, so that the customer believes that they are really getting a good deal when they are not, than the practice is unethical.

Some other forms of unethical pricing strategies are price discrimination and predatory pricing. **Price discrimination** occurs when a company charges different amounts for a product in different situations. For example, consider a customer that walks into a store and casually chooses a few items to purchase and another customer who, for some reason, urgently needed the same products. It would be unethical price discriminate if when they checked out, the manager, noticing their different needs for the product, charged the customer with an urgent need twice the amount he charged the other customer.

Predatory pricing is a practice of providing goods at lower prices than competitors in order to drive competitors out of business. For example, if one business can make a product at a lower cost than their competitors can, and chooses to sell it at a cost below their competitors, driving them out of business. This is not necessarily unethical, it is feasible that something like this would occur naturally. However, if once the competitors are removed from the market the original company chooses to raise their prices above what the previous prices were, it would be unethical. For a company that is large and has many locations it is actually illegal for them to practice price discrimination by lowering prices in a single store in order to drive competitors in that area out of business (in other words, they cannot use price discrimination as a form of predatory pricing).

Dumping is another unethical pricing strategy that companies can adopt. Dumping is when a company sells a large number of products at a price below the fair value. Typically dumping occurs when a company exports their product. They will sell a large amount in a foreign market at a price far below what they would sell them for in domestic markets (markets in the country that they are based in). This essentially gives them a monopoly in the foreign market and drives competitors out of business. Meanwhile they can maintain the same profits in domestic markets.

It is also possible for the ethics of a product itself to come into question. The marketing of products that are considered to be hazardous or dangerous is often criticized. Another factor is when products are poorly made. If customers believe that the products that a company manufactures are unreasonably poorly made than they will most likely develop an opinion of the company being unethical and cheating their customers. This would lead to them not buying other products from the company, and most likely spreading the opinion. Another way that customers could perceive a company as being unethical is if they produce and market products that they know will quickly become obsolete. This sort of problem is easily seen in the technology industry where the technological abilities and capacities change at a rapid rate. If a company is purposely heavily marketing products as the best and newest when they know that they will soon be obsolete and just want to make a profit, than the practice is unethical.

In the United States, accounting fraud in its many forms is the most common type of fraud. Some examples of accounting fraud include the Enron scandal (in which Enron was discovered to hide massive debt using special purpose entities) or the Tyco scandal (in which the chief executives of Tyco were discovered to have stolen millions of dollars from the company). In each example the problem involved deception that related to the company's financial statements. Accountants face increasing pressures to ensure that financial statements show a company in favorable light which increases the risk of accounting fraud. Therefore, accounts must adhere to a strict set of ethical standards and comply with standardized accounting methods.

Consumer fraud is also an important factor in business. Consumer fraud occurs when consumers or customers work to deceive businesses for their own gain. For example, if a customer switches the price tags on a product so that they pay less, it would be consumer fraud. Shoplifting is also considered to be a type of consumer fraud. Businesses that operate with a policy of believing that "the customer is always right" (or the philosophy that the interests of the customer should be considered most important) often find that they are taken advantage of by customers and have to employ stricter return policies or other restrictions to protect themselves. This can be found in major department stores that put a barcode sticker on top of a UPC on a product such as make-up. This is then scanned into the computer so if it is returned, it will be linked to the transaction in which it was purchased.

There are a number of different ways and types of information that businesses collect. For example, ad hoc reporting is one kind of information that businesses can use. Ad hoc is a Latin term which literally means "for this." This is basically what ad hoc reporting is used for. Ad hoc reporting involves gathering information for a specific purpose, such as filling a hole in a financial statement or trying to decide which product will be more popular. In any case, it is information compiled to answer a specific question.

PROTECTING AND STEALING PROPRIETARY INFORMATION

Another type of information that is important in business is proprietary information. Put most simply, proprietary information refers to information which a company keeps confidential. More specifically, proprietary information is information which is believed to give the company a competitive advantage and which is the property of the proprietor (be that a single owner or many). Proprietary information can also be referred to as trade secrets. The control of proprietary information is another example of a way in which information is essential to successful business practices.

For example, financial information is often considered proprietary information. Although all publicly traded companies are required by law to publish financial statements each year, they by no means make all of the financial information they collect available to the public. Financial information which could be proprietary includes profit margins, budgets, sales goals and other information. Another type of proprietary information is marketing information. Information such as marketing strategy or information about new products coming to market, for example, would be proprietary information. A third type of proprietary information is research information.

This would include secret formulas or recipes that a company uses, information about the development of new technologies, problems that a company is facing in development or their progress in developing certain technologies. The control of proprietary information is very important to the success of a business. Consider if every company knew exactly what their competitor's secret formulas, financial situation and marketing strategies were. It would be nearly impossible for businesses to thrive and it is therefore essential that businesses maintain control of their proprietary information.

There are a few ways in which companies work to maintain control of proprietary information. For example, non-disclosure agreements (which can also be called proprietary information agreements) are one method of protecting proprietary information. Another way that companies protect themselves is with non-competition agreement. While non-disclosure agreements work to ensure that information is not spread around, non-competition agreements are signed between owners and employees with access to information to ensure that they will not use information that they gain to enter into competition with the business. Businesses also work to ensure that they have security (both electronic and otherwise) to stop the information from being stolen.

To a lesser extent there are also ways in which trade secrets are protected by law. Trade secrets have come to be classified under laws which protect patents, copyrights and trademarks. In other words, if a company can show that the proprietary information fits the legal description of a trade secret (that is, that the company takes reasonable steps to keep it confidential and it has some sort of economic value), it is protected under intellectual-property rights laws.

For this reason, ethics involving proprietary information is closely related to the legal rights associated with intellectual-property rights. The other types of intellectual property rights – patents, copyrights and trademarks – also have specific sets of qualifications which must be met. A patent can only be obtained for information which a person or business can prove is new and non-obvious. In other words, they must have actually invented something. A copyright covers materials that are written. A trademark refers to words or names that can be identified with specific companies and products. For example, logos, symbols and brand names are all types of trademarks.

As businesses attempt to protect proprietary information it opens up a whole other section of ethics which relates to those who would attempt to discover than information. The field of information gathering about companies can take two different forms. It can be considered corporate intelligence and corporate espionage.

Corporate intelligence describes the ethical and legal end of information gathering. A corporate intelligence agent may search publicly available online information about a company, follow their moves in the news and other media, conduct interviews with employees (after truthfully disclosing who they are), look into court documents from cases the company has been involved in, conduct studies or surveys of customers or gather information in any other legal way. The key point in ensuring that the information gathering is legal is that the information is publicly available, it just may take time and energy to compile and analyze it all. Essentially corporate intelligence involves researching a company to better understand them and then using that information to gain a competitive advantage. Often corporate intelligence is gathered for the purpose of benchmarking how the company should be performing.

Corporate intelligence is used for two different purposes: strategic intelligence and tactical intelligence. Strategic intelligence is information gathering that has its purpose in the long run success of the business. For example, information that is used to help the company determine what its goals should be for growth and sales in the future, or to help them better understand what possible challenges they may face as they attempt to expand. Tactical intelligence, on the other hand, is used to help the company make short term decisions. It is based in helping the company quickly understand their competitiveness and to gain a larger market share. For example, it is important to know what types of products competitors are offering and how they are similar or different than the products being offered by other companies. Monitoring the price that competitors charge for their products and the areas where they are marketing most heavily also falls under tactical intelligence.

CORPORATE ESPIONAGE

Corporate espionage is the unethical and illegal side of information gathering. While corporate intelligence focuses on the gathering of publicly available information, corporate espionage is based in discovering proprietary information and trade secrets through more unethical means. Especially with the rise of the internet, hacking has become an increasingly popular way for people to gain access to information about a business. Some other popular methods of corporate espionage include dumpster diving, physically copying information from a hard drive, social engineering, bribery and attempting to hire the company's key employees.

Hacking is the process of breaking into computers or networks. There are three basic types of hacking: system hacking, remote hacking and physical hacking. System hacking occurs when a lower level employee who already has access to a company's network takes advantage of their position and hacks into higher levels of security within the database in order to collect information. Remote hacking occurs when a person who is not affiliated with the company and has no access to their information attempts to gain higher or administrative access.

Typically remote hacking is done over the internet. For example, one way this could be done is through a company's website. If the website is routinely updated with information from a company's database then the hacker could attempt to get past the firewall and into the database, and from their access the rest of the company's information. Physical hacking requires that the hacker physically enter the place of business. This could be used if they were to simply walk into a company and look for an empty desk. They could then sit down and use that employee's workstation to gain access to sensitive information. Another form of physical hacking could involve the hackers finding the company's server and use a protocol analyzer somewhere that it wouldn't be easily found in order to steal data such as passwords, names, phone numbers or memos.

Dumpster diving in terms of corporate espionage involves literally going through a company's trash in an attempt to gather information. Though it is becoming less common for companies to simply throw away copies of proprietary information because they are aware of the possibility of this tactic, even simple things such as copies of memos or letterheads can give corporate espionage agents valuable information about possible ways to gain information in the future. For example, they can learn how to send legitimate looking, but false, memos or letters or learn about people to possibly impersonate as.

Social engineering is essentially similar to hacking, but on a personal level instead of a software level. While hackers work to infiltrate a company through its software, websites or networks, social engineers work with people to try and learn information about a company. It involves an attempt to trick individuals so as to gain access to or learn valuable information. For example, shoulder surfing is a common type of social engineering. Shoulder surfing is when a person looks over a person's shoulder and watches them type in their password.

This way they can later use that person's identification information to gain access to the system. Although it is less sophisticated, password guessing is another common form of social engineering. Employees and just people in general are counseled more and more often to include various numbers and symbols in addition to words in their passwords in order to make this type of social engineering less feasible. If people just use names or important dates as their passwords than it makes it easy for a social engineer to do a little research about the person and guess their password.

Social engineering doesn't even necessarily have to involve learning an employee's passwords. It could also involve a person calling an employee, manager or executive and asking them about their personal information and passwords under the guise of needing access in order to complete important system work for the company. Another example could be a person calling an employee under the guise of being a company executive and asking them to divulge company information.

A social engineer need not actually come into contact with the people from which they steal information. For example, a social engineer attempting to guess an employee's password may be able to determine information about them through social media sites or other sources. Two other common methods of social engineering that do not require the person to come into contact with employees are whacking and phone eavesdropping. Whacking is wireless hacking. If a company uses wireless networks and the person can gain access to it then they can gain access to company information. They can spy on any correspondence or files that are accessed over the network with ease because information sent within the network is rarely encrypted. Phone eavesdropping can include listening in on phone calls or monitoring a fax line. In any case, all forms of social engineering are unethical because they involve deceit and trickery.

BLUFFING

The discussion of protecting proprietary information brings up another issue: bluffing. If companies work to ensure that information does not get made public, and if controlling information can be a great benefit to a business, then the problem becomes determining how much information a business should be willing to share with other in negotiations. The debate over whether bluffing is ethical is ongoing. On the one hand, there are many that believe that bluffing is a form of lying and should be considered universally unethical. Indeed, in many cases excessive bluffing and deception can be a large hindrance to the progression of negotiations and just make it more difficult for all involved. It can also cause a bad reputation to be formed of an executive or company that would have a negative effect.

There are also many people that believe that business should be held to slightly different standards of ethics than a private individual would be. This view considered business to be similar to a game in which strategy, in this case bluffing, would be required for success. This viewpoint emphasizes the role of an executive. Namely, it is the job of executives to maximize the company's profits (and it is typically in their own personal best interest to do so). Allowing the free spreading of the company's information would not be a very effective way of doing this. It makes sense than a businessperson should feel obliged to in many cases to not share all of the information available to them, and to bluff where necessary to achieve the best outcome for the company.

CONFLICTS OF INTEREST

A conflict of interest is when a person has multiple interests and they influence each other. One way to think of a person having multiple interests is to think of a person having multiple "roles." If a person is a police officer and a relative is being tried for a crime, they would likely not be allowed to work on the case because it gives them an opportunity to exploit their role as a police officer to benefit them in their family role. In the example, the person has two roles, a police officer and a family member. Therefore it would be considered a conflict of interest.

An example would be if a government official owns stock and is asked to vote on laws regarding the stock market. This would be a conflict of interest because it puts them in a situation where their interests as a stock owner and their interests as a public official are both relevant. It would be natural for the official to consider both roles in making his decision and therefore it is a conflict of interest because the two roles influence each other. A conflict of interest does not necessarily mean that someone has or will exploit their role, but that they are in a position to.

There are a number of different types of conflict of interest. One type is a self-dealing conflict of interest. This occurs when a person is part of (or benefits from) both ends of a deal. For example, if an official used government money to hire a business which they owned for a project. If the official chooses their own business not because it is the most cost effective or high quality option (which is a highly subjective decision), but simply because they own it and wish to collect the profits, then it would be unethical and a conflict of interest. The official is allowing their roles as a businessperson and a government official to both influence their decision.

Another type of conflict of interest is an outside employment conflict of interest. With this type of conflict of interest a person has multiple jobs and their interest conflicts between them. For example, if a person were to work for two different firms which were both working to develop the same type of product there would be a clear conflict of interest that was resulting from their outside employment. There would be a temptation to use information gleaned in one of the businesses to either help or mislead the other business (whichever would be more beneficial to the employee at the time). They would not be able to do their work ethically or properly under such circumstances.

Accepting gifts from friends that a person does business with could be a conflict of interest. Family interest refers to considering the interests of family ahead of what is truly best for the business. It can occur in terms of hiring, firing, promoting, employment benefits or other factors. If a person were to promote their family interests ahead of the interests of their company it would be called nepotism.

Another type of conflict of interest is called pump and dump. This happens when a broker owns securities and spreads rumors about them to make the price go up. Then they sell them before the price goes back down.

In addition, not all types of conflicts of interest have to fit into one of those categories. For example, any organization which is self-policing (or in charge of creating regulations and policies that determine how it may function) would be a conflict of interest. There is a lot of room for the organization to consider its own best benefits and not necessarily how to best fulfill its role when it is self-policing. It could also become a conflict of interest if a manager were told that they would receive a bonus at the end of each year to the amount that they were under the company's budget. This would give the incentive to purchase cheaply made supplies which could risk the safety or impair the efficiency of employees.

INSIDER TRADING

Insider trading also has important ethical consideration in business. Insider trading describes when a company's insider (who are considered to be any official or owner who possesses ten percent or more of the company's stock) buy or sell stock. Insider trading can occur in ways that are legal or illegal. Legal insider trading occurs when a person legally trades stock within their own company. To prevent insiders from trading stock often, they are restricted from buying and selling stock within a six month period.

This way they make their stock decisions on a basis of how they believe that the company will perform long term. To trade legally, insiders must also report their trades to the SEC within two business days. Illegal insider trading occurs when an insider gains information about the company which is not available to the public and considers that information in buying stock. Insider trading can apply to not just the insider, but also their friends, family or employees who have access to nonpublic information. Any person who gives a tip to an outsider and shares nonpublic information that could influence their trading decisions could also be accused of insider trading.

EMPLOYEE MONITORING

Another ethical issue involves monitoring within the working environment. Growing technology has made it ever easier for employers to monitor employees, which is beneficial to them as it allows them increased control over productivity.

However, privacy laws do place limits on the extent to which employers may monitor their workers. For example, in most cases it is not appropriate for an employer to inquire as to what their employees are doing off the job unless the behavior is damaging to the company or illegal.

However, drug testing would be a different story. Although in some professions (those which are deemed to have safety concerns involved) random drug testing is allowed, in other's drug testing is allowed only upon application or with reasonable cause. Also, an employer does not have the right to request or demand that an employee, or potential employee, take a lie detector test.

In many cases, even if the activities of an employee are illegal the employer does not have the right to inquire about them. The exception would be if the employer has a legitimate reason to believe that the actions are impairing the employee's ability to perform their job.

There are a few exceptions to the rule. Ronald Reagan's Executive Order 12564 and the Drug-Free Workplace Act of 1998 impacted the treatment of employees of the federal government. These employees are to be held to a higher standard and are excepted to abstain from illegal drugs and substances while on and off the job.

However, there are ways that employers can monitor their employee's off-duty behavior. For example, postings on social media sites are openly available. An employer can even hire a third party to monitor postings by employees on the grounds that if they post information that is either confidential or damaging to the company it would be legal for the employer to act on it. An employer also has the right to know if an employee is working multiple jobs.

This way that can better ensure that there is not a conflict of interest or that scheduling conflicts do not arise. Also, because it is illegal to discriminate on a basis of religious or political beliefs, employers are not allowed to enquire about an employee's beliefs (if, however, the employee displays their beliefs in the workplace the employer may reprimand them). As a rule of thumb, employers really don't have many rights to inquire about any off duty behaviors unless they impair the employee's ability to work. For example, if an employee demonstrates chronic absenteeism (being absent from work) the employer may not have the right to ask about where they go or what they do, but they would have the right to fire them if they are clearly in violation of their responsibilities to the company.

It is also important that the privacy of employees be maintained in other ways. For example, if a business pays its employees through direct deposit then it is important that the business ensures that the employees' financial information is kept confidential. Identity theft by those with access to the information could become a concern. If the company has a health insurance policy and keeps medical records of all the employees, assuming that an employee does not have any serious health concerns, these records should only be available to the person directly responsible for administering and overseeing the policy in order to maintain privacy.

In terms of actual on the job behaviors employers have far more rights. For example, setting dress and grooming standards is perfectly allowable. Also, there are few laws restricting the use of cameras in workplaces (although audio recorders are more restricted because they may fall under wiretapping and eavesdropping laws). In part, this is because in addition to helping them monitor employees, video cameras are a way of preventing theft or of ensuring employee safety. Employers also have the right to monitor phone calls made from company phones (including messages left on voicemail). In addition, if an employee wears a headset as part of their job their employer does have the right to monitor anything that they say into it.

Employers also have the right to monitor web activity of employees and monitor an employee's terminal. Because the computers and networks are all owned by the company, anything that an employee does is subject to surveillance. This helps employers ensure that employees are not misusing resources, wasting time or visiting inappropriate sites. Employers can see what is currently on their employees' screens and any material saved on their computers. They can even track the keystrokes that an employee makes to see how much work they are doing or what they are typing. Although some employers do notify their employees that they are being monitored, it is not strictly required and the employee cannot always tell. In some occupations employers may even use keystroke monitors which track the number of keystrokes an employee uses in a given amount of time. The employer's rights also extend to any emails or other types of messages sent over the company's network, even messages that are marked as personal or private. Even once an email has been deleted it is still in the system.

With the proliferation of internet businesses and advertising it is increasingly easy for businesses to monitor both their employees and their customers. Some important terms to be aware of are spam, virus and cookie. Spam is when a person (or business) sends out large amounts of electronic messages indiscriminately. Essentially it is an attempt to flood the internet with a copy of a message so that it is seen by as many people as possible, without them soliciting the information. While spam is typically thought of in terms of email, it also applies to other electronic situations such as instant messages, chat rooms or blogs.

A virus is a piece of code (not software) which is used to disrupt computer function. It can do this by deleting information, slowing a computer down, damaging programs or through other methods. Though some viruses are mild, they can also be quite destructive. Viruses attach themselves to files and travel from computer to computer. Once the file is activated on a computer, so is the virus.

A cookie is a piece of software used so that a site (called the origin site) can send information to a computer's browser and vice versa. Typically cookies are used to track a user's information and for personalization. For example, one type of cookie is a shopping cart on an internet store. The shopping cart keeps track of the information describing the products the person is buying so that they can continue to shop. Cookies can also be used so that a site will remember a person's preferences across multiple visits. For example, on Google a person can select the number of responses they want shown per page, and it will be the same the next time they search. Another use of cookies is in remembering passwords. With some sites a person has to log on only once, and they will still be logged on the next time that they visit the site. This is because of a cookie. Cookies can therefore be used to track customers and employees activities.

In addition to these various types of monitoring it is important that customers, employees and even employers be aware of privacy laws regarding government access to information. The Privacy Act of 1974 was passed in order to protect the privacy of individuals as it related to the government's ability to gather information. According to the act, a person has the right to know about and access any files that the federal government is keeping on them that is in a system of records (meaning it is attached to their name, social security number or other type identifier). In addition, a person may request corrections to documents that are incomplete or incorrect. The act also prevents government agencies from sharing information they have gathered with other agencies, or from anyone but the individual which the information concerns.

In some ways, many people consider the USA PATRIOT Act (Patriot Act) to be in conflict with the Privacy Act because it allows the government a wide license to gather information. In an attempt to protect against terrorism, the Patriot Act (in some cases) allows the FBI to search the email, phone records, and financial records of citizens, as well as search their homes or offices without their knowledge. This violates the portion or the Privacy Act which dictates that a person should be aware of government records kept on them.

 Business Organization and Ethics

After considering the many different forms of ethics, it becomes necessary to consider the question of whether a business can actually be considered to have responsibilities. There are three basic ways in which a business can be organized: as a proprietorship, partnership or corporation. To explain it simply, in a proprietorship there is one owner of the business. When the business does well it reflects in the proprietor's (owner's) finances, and when it does poorly the same occurs. From a legal standpoint the proprietor is essentially connected to what this business does. Therefore, it follows that the actions of the business fall back to the morality of the proprietor. (This isn't to say however that individual employees are free of guilt when they act unethically, just that from an overall standpoint of business decisions as a whole, the proprietor is responsible for the direction the company takes.)

A partnership is run essentially the same way as a proprietorship, but with multiple owners. Thus the profits and failings are fundamentally connected to the finances of the partners. Of course it is quite a bit more involved as far as paperwork goes, and strict descriptions of individual roles and responsibilities of the different partners are required. However, as with a proprietorship, the actions of the business can be considered to fall to the morality of the partners.

A corporation becomes even more complicated than a partnership. A corporation does not have a single owner, but rather it has many shareholders. Instead of having a clear owner, corporations are led by an elected board of directors which is responsible for appointing people to oversee daily operations of the business, such as managers and various corporate officers. Because of this setup, from a legal standpoint, the shareholders (who would be considered the owners of a corporation) do not have a direct responsibility for the finances or daily actions of the company because they do not necessarily decide them.

The board of directors on the other hand does have a legal responsibility for the actions of the company, but they do not always have an ownership interest. The board of directors holds legal responsibility for the success of the firm and use of its assets, however they rarely control the day to day management of the firm. Rather, the board meets a few times a year and the managers and corporate officers oversee the actual day to day workings of the business.

Clearly, it becomes harder to pinpoint where the responsibility for the overall ethics of the company can be said to lie, or where it originates from because there are so many different pertinent groups within the organization. Going further, some people question if even the corporation itself be considered to have moral structures. Some theories believe that the corporation itself can be attributed a certain moral structure, based on the way the internal communications and operations are set up.

What it comes down to is that no matter how the company is set up, it is fairly universally accepted that businesses do in fact have certain responsibilities.

 Business Regulations & Entities

There are two basic ways that ethics within business can be regulated: voluntary practices and mandated boundaries. Voluntary practices are the ethical practices of a business that are not required, or that the business engages in by choice. Voluntary practices can include the values and beliefs of a business that guide the way that they interact with their employees or customers. These practices are mandated from within the business to ensure that employees and managers are acting in ways that are not harmful to the company or its reputation.

For example, many businesses have what are called core practices. Core practices are the basic, day to day best practices of the company. In other words, the core practices are the accepted way of doing things in the business that are just the best way to get them done as best as possible. For example, if a company has a reputation for high quality, a core practice of the business may be that every order is double checked for correctness before being shipped to a customer.

Another example of a voluntary practice would be joining the Better Business Bureau (BBB). The BBB is a self-regulatory body which businesses may become a member of (although the BBB is nonprofit, member businesses do have to pay dues). The BBB helps both business and consumers by helping provide information that helps consumers make good decisions. They also provide programs to help companies ensure that their advertising and sales are being done ethically. The BBB also works as a mediator in disputes. They will provide directions for the company in handling disputes with customers and reviews the case. Their main focus is to ensure that businesses are conforming to legal requirements, as well as basic societal expectations and norms. However, the BBB works on a voluntary basis and does not have the power to force members to do things.

Businesses will also typically engage in some sort of philanthropy. Philanthropy is basically just charity or service work. In other words, philanthropy is giving back to the community. For example, philanthropy could consist of a company donating money to a local charity. However, it could also include a company donating goods, such as a restaurant catering an event for free, or a clothing store donating clothes to a homeless shelter.

In addition to these voluntary practices, there are also government regulations which influence the ways that businesses can or can't behave. These government regulations fall under the category of mandated boundaries. In addition to government regulations, mandated boundaries include all laws, rules, regulations and requirements imposed on businesses from external sources. Regulations applying to businesses often change as public opinion changes. This can occur because there is a large scale shift in the general opinion of the population, because of the specific opinion of a particular judge, because new information about the safety of a practice develops or any number of different reasons.

Laws in general are typically divided into one of two categories: criminal laws and civil laws. A criminal law is enforced by government agencies (such as police) and is typically passed to prohibit actions, such as fraud or theft. In addition, violators of criminal laws are also subject to punishments ranging from fines, to prison or jail sentences, to capital punishment.

Civil laws deal with a person, organization or businesses' rights and responsibilities. Civil cases never involve a government agency prosecuting a person for breaking a law. In civil cases one person (or organization) believes that another has in some way violated their rights and they take them to court for compensation. This compensation can take many forms, such as a refund or an award for a certain amount of money or a court order to perform services. When a person does this, it is called suing. For example, consider a lawn mowing company that was hired to mow a person's lawn, had the customer pay in advance, and then never came to mow their lawn. The person may sue for a refund of the money that they had paid the company. They could also sue for additional costs in excess of what they would have paid that they had to pay to find a new company to mow the lawn. The court may also simply order the company to mow the lawn as previously agreed.

Although the federal government never prosecutes people in civil cases (that would make it a criminal case) there are a few instances in which the federal government does get involved in civil cases. One of the rare examples would be if a hospital were overbilling on Medicare. Because Medicare is paid through the federal government, the federal government would sue the hospital in a civil case.

The majority of cases involving business ethics end up being civil cases, however there are various criminal laws which come into play as well. For example, insider trading cases are criminal cases. Insider trading is a violation of federal law and cases of it are investigated and prosecuted by the Security Exchange Commission (SEC), a government agency. Because insider trading does involve criminal law, a person can be sent to jail if they are convicted.

The types of laws and regulations which apply to business typically fall into certain categories: laws regulating competition, protecting consumers and ensuring equality and safety.

MARKET COMPETITION AND MONOPOLIES

Among the earliest laws to regulate business in the United States were those regulating market competition. These laws were called antitrust laws (now they are given the name procompetitive legislation). They were designed to prevent monopolies from forming which were harmful to the economy as a whole. To better understand the significance of laws regulating competition, it is important to understand the terms market, monopoly and economy.

The most basic use of the word market is to describe a physical location where goods are bought and sold. For example, a supermarket is where people can go to buy groceries and other products. A person may say that they are going to the market. This is a correct use of the term. However, online stores or action sites are also considered markets, necessitating a slightly broader definition. Market can also be used more abstractly to refer to the people who buy a particular product. The markets for apples or oranges, for example, could refer to the number of people who wish to buy apples or oranges or to the number of apples and oranges that these people wish to buy. In this sense, markets can be considered in local or global terms as is relevant. The owner of a grocery store in a small town would need to know about the market for bread in that specific town. On a slightly larger scale, a camping supply store found in various locations around Wyoming may wish to know about the market for camping supplies in Oregon if they are considering expanding. Going larger still, people are greatly affected when there are large shifts in the nation's housing market. Finally, a member of the United Nations may need to learn more about the worldwide market for crude oil.

The term market is closely related to the term economy. Most simply an economy can be described as a conglomeration of all of the different markets. Economies are considered over a geographic area, though the area being considered can vary in size. Most often people consider economies in terms of countries. For example, a person studying the United States' economy may look at factors such as Gross Domestic Product (GDP), different types of goods bought and sold (and whether they are agricultural goods, technological or services, etc.), manufacturing data, labor statistics, natural resources, the success of different types of businesses and many other factors. Economics is the study of economies.

Returning to the concept of a monopoly, a monopoly occurs when a single person or business is the only supplier of a particular product. Originally the railroads were a large monopoly. Essentially while there may have been small or localized railroads, there was only one railroad company which had the resources and ability to transport in a large scale across different parts of the country. Therefore, farmers were forced to ship their produce using this railroad. Of course, knowing that it the farmers were dependent, the railroads were able to charge whatever they wanted. The increase of price would of course translate to higher prices on agricultural products, and lower profits for the farmers as they tried to keep prices competitive. It would affect not only the farmers however, but also the stores that eventually bought and sold the goods and also anyone who bought the produce. Therefore, the monopoly was detrimental to the economy as a whole.

As a more modern example, imagine that one day a company that manufactured hard drives bought out every other company in the world that manufactured hard drives. For the sake of argument, assume that no one has the resources to start up a new hard drive manufacturing business. Because everyone is so dependent on computers and computers have to have hard drives, the business could cause a huge increase in the price of computers and people would still buy them. Because people would spend more money on a computer they would have less money to buy food or pay their bills. The entertainment industry would also suffer. Therefore, to prevent monopolies from developing there is procompetitive legislation which regulates competition through preventing monopolies and encouraging competition among companies in a market. For example, some of these laws prohibit unfair or deceptive acts (Wheeler-Lea Act), protect trademarks and brand names (Lanham Act), punish dealing in counterfeit goods (Trademark Counterfeiting Act) and prohibit price discrimination and exclusive dealing (Clayton Act).

In addition to laws which encourage competition, businesses are also regulated through laws that protect consumers. The first consumer protection law was the Pure Food and Drug Act passed in 1906. The law was passed in response to public uproar about the unsafe practices in the meat packing industry. The industry practiced virtually no sanitation and gave little thought to the actual safety of the product when selling it to consumers. Over time, many laws have been passed which force companies to consider safety and fairness to consumers with their products, to provide accurate information about the products that they are selling or providing and to follow required safety and sanitation practices.

The Federal Trade Commission (FTC) is responsible for enforcing consumer protection laws. More generally, the FTC is responsible for regulating any economic issue which affects the average citizen. For example, the original purpose of the FTC was to prevent unfair or anticompetitive methods used by companies. The FTC's Bureau of Consumer Protection more specifically works to protect consumers from unfair business practices by regulating advertising and marketing (for example, the FTC requires a standard of truth in advertising), finances (for example, the truth in lending act is enforced by the FTC) and protecting privacy among other things.

For example, the Children's Online Privacy Protection Act (COPPA) is enforced by the FTC and prevents companies from obtaining personal information from children under 13 without their parent's consent. The FTC also enforces rules regulating Do Not Call Lists from telemarketers. One of the primary ways which the Bureau of Consumer Protection works to protect consumers is by ensuring free and available information about products – such as the care labels on clothes and the availability of free credit reports every year.

Some specific laws that protect consumers may control the labeling of hazardous household substances (Federal Hazardous substances Labeling Act), allow the government to recall dangerous toys (Toy Safety Act) and require nutritional information on all processed foods (Nutritional Labeling and Education Act).

TITLE VII

The final set of laws that regulate businesses are those which promote equality and safety. When it comes to equality, the primary law involved is Title VII of the Civil Rights Act of 1964. According to Title VII a person may not be discriminated against based on their race, color, religion, gender or nationality. The applications of the law are fairly straightforward, a business cannot refuse to hire someone, or do business with someone, on a basis of any of those factors. In cases where the business can prove that, for example, that the job can only be done by a specific gender then it is allowed (however, exceptions cannot be applied on a basis of race).

The Civil Rights Act also created the Equal Employment Opportunities Commission (EEOC). The EEOC was created to ensure that the Civil Rights Act was enforced, and conduct investigations in cases where there may be violations.

AFFIRMATIVE ACTION

The EEOC also helps in the implementation of programs which promote equality involving the areas mentioned in the Civil Rights Act. These programs are called affirmative action programs. Affirmative action basically describes programs which seek to reduce or reverse the effects of discrimination, as opposed to merely "not practicing" it.

The term affirmative action was first used by President Kennedy in stating that federal money used be used to "take affirmative action" in ending discrimination. Shortly after, the Civil Rights Act was passed and signed by President Johnson. President Johnson described the idea behind affirmative action by comparing life to a race. He said that you cannot take a person who has been chained up for years and, putting them at the starting line of a race, believe it to have been fair. Although the term affirmative action can be used to apply to any form of discrimination (such as gender or age), most often people consider and use it in terms of discrimination based on race or color.

Affirmative action programs have been applied not only to workplace discrimination, but also to education as well. Many universities began practicing policies designed to increase the number of minority students attending the university. While there is support for such programs, affirmative action programs have also faced a wide amount of criticism.

In one famous case, Regents of the University of California vs. Bakke, Allan Bakke sued a medical school he had been applying to for rejecting his application multiple times. Allan Bakke was white and the school had set quotas dictating that at least 16 of the applicants admitted must be of minority races. Although Bakke could prove that his admittance criteria were better than the accepted minority applicants, the minority applicants were accepted so that the school could meet its quota. Bakke claimed that this was a violation of the Equal Protection Clause of the Fourteenth Amendment. The Supreme Court ruled in his favor 5-4, deciding that although the school could consider race as an acceptance criteria, the strict guideline of a specific numerical quota was not allowable. As time progresses, businesses and universities continue to look for ways of both implementing affirmative action programs and not creating "reverse discrimination" against the minority group.

COMPARABLE WORTH

Another equality issue which aims at correcting past injustices is comparable worth. Virtually all statistics show that even today the average female worker makes only about two thirds of what the average male worker does. The theory of comparable worth is that this is a result of widespread past discrimination against women. The idea is that jobs typically held by women receive lower pay on average than jobs typically held by men because those jobs were devalued in the past. Advocates of comparable worth work to ensure that jobs typically held by women that involve the same levels of work and risk as other jobs, receive the same level of pay.

Other examples of laws promoting equality ensure equal pay for men and women working the same jobs (Equal Pay Act), prohibit discrimination based on age (Age Discrimination in Employment Act) and prohibit discrimination based on pregnancy or related medical conditions (Pregnancy Discrimination Act).

ADA

There are also many other laws in addition to the Civil Rights Act which address issues of equality. For example, the Americans with Disabilities Act (ADA) which is designed to ensure that people with disabilities receive the same opportunities for work as people without disabilities. The act applies to all government agencies and labor unions. The law also extends to private employers with more than 15 employees. Within a workplace the law can be applied to practices such as hiring employees, firing employees and promoting employees. For example, under the ADA a business may be required to install a ramp leading to the front doors to ensure that employees confined to a wheelchair are equally able to work. This sort of practice is referred to as reasonable accommodation, and it is required under the law. Another example of reasonable accommodation could be purchasing a specialized machine that could be used by a blind employee. The law does not require that any sort of preferential treatment be given to disabled employees or applicants. An employee is free to choose to hire the most skilled employee and fire the least skilled employee based on the qualifications required for a job.

OSHA

Many laws also focus on protecting the safety of employees. For example, the Occupational Safety and Health Administration (OSHA) was created to ensure that business employ proper safety methods and maintain safe working conditions. It specifically protects workers against workplace hazards. For example, it dictates that moving parts must be covered so that a worker couldn't happen to contact it and injure themselves, sets limits on the amount of chemical that a worker can be exposed to, regulates the use of protective equipment for dangerous work environments and many other aspects of worker safety as well.

EPA

Safety laws also extend to the environment. Specifically, the Environmental Protection Agency (EPA) was created to ensure that environmental laws were followed. For example, some environmental safety laws mandate air quality standards (Clean Air Act), protect endangered plants and animals (Endangered Species Act), reduce and eliminate water pollution (Federal Water Pollution Control Act) and address the EPA's ability to respond to oil spills (Oil Pollution Act).

FDA

Another regulatory agency which is meant to protect consumers is the Food and Drug Administration. The Food and Drug Administration, or FDA, is a regulatory agency which reports to the United States Department of Health and Human Services and employs over 11,000 people. It is the responsibility of the FDA to ensure public health and safety. They do this by monitoring many products which come into contact with people, and ensuring that they are safe, sanitary and properly labeled. Their influence includes food, drugs, vaccines, cosmetics, blood transfusions and radioactive products. However, there are things that the FDA does not regulate, including illegal drugs (which are regulated by the Drug Enforcement Agency), consumer products such as toys and appliances and the advertising of products (although the FDA does regulate advertising of tobacco and prescription drugs).

The FDA is in place to ensure that businesses and manufacturers do not cut corners with potentially dangerous products. The origins of the FDA can be traced to the Pure Food and Drug Act of 1906 which worked to counter diseases and sicknesses which resulted in the lack sanitation practices by food producing industries.

SA8000

SA8000 is a certification provided by Social Accountability International (SAI) that encourages companies and organizations to develop and maintain socially acceptable practices in the workplace. It focuses on compliance in eight major areas:

- child labor
- forced labor
- health and safety
- free association and collective bargaining
- discrimination
- disciplinary practices
- working hours
- compensation

Employee Relations

With the average workweek at forty or more hours a week there is a lot of room for problems to arise in the workplace. Ergonomics is meant to make workers more productive. It is the study of designing more comfortably or easily used equipment. With ergonomics, a person's working environment is altered to suit them instead of the person having to adapt to their environment. The goals that ergonomics works to fulfill are increasing health and productivity. If a person is in a comfortable work environment it is easier for them to work and problems such as carpel tunnel can be avoided.

However, most issues that arise in workplaces involve relations between the employer and employees. The relationship between employer and employee is meant to be a mutually beneficial one, employees are provided with a job and pay and employers are provided with someone to fill the position. However, the issue of employment is often fraught with ethical issues. For example, recently the idea of a "new social contract" has been popularized.

During the 17th and 18th centuries, the theory of a social contract between governments and people became popularized. Similarly, in modern times there has been a type of unwritten social contract between employers and employees. If workers were loyal, punctual and at least decently efficient they could expect to keep their jobs and perhaps even advance over time. However, the world has entered into a new era with a new social contract. In many cases, the old contract created cost inefficient working environments with little incentive for improvement. In some cases, improvements in technology have made certain jobs unnecessary, resulting in people losing the jobs they expected to have consistently.

Downsizing to eliminate unnecessary jobs also does this. The "new" social contract of the workplace requires an employee to work to the best of their ability, increase their knowledge, improve over time and be loyal and ethical in their work. There are also expectations that employees have for their employment. For example, honesty from employers (they shouldn't go looking for a person's replacement behind their back if they have not told the employee that their work is unsatisfactory), occasional pay raises and other benefits.

Human Resource Management (HRM) is a field involving the management of employees and includes everything from hiring practices to training programs to benefit programs to prevent employees from quitting. On factor in HRM is determining the needs of a company. Considering how many employees are needed and what their specific responsibilities should be is a part of this. Another factor of HRM is attracting employees, or hiring them. Once employees are selected the focus of HRM shifts to ensuring that they are aware of their duties and capable of executing them. This may require training or orientation programs, employee development and regular performance appraisals. The final factor that HRM focuses on is retaining employees. This requires considering things such as wages, benefits packages and opportunities for promotion.

Minimum Wage

One important difficulty that deserves mention in the category of employer-employee relations is wage issues. The idea of a **"living wage"** was first introduced in the 1920's. The term living wage is used to describe a wage that is sufficient to allow education, good health and eventually retirement. In other words, the living wage is intended to be met through the minimum wage laws that are in force today.

Minimum wage was instituted in the late 1930's during the Great Depression. During this time workers were making only pennies an hour and the standard of living had plummeted. This was especially true for female or child laborers. They were considered to be substandard workers and were therefore given substandard wages. In 1938 the minimum hourly wage was set by the government at twenty five cents. The laws are still in effect and as cost of living and other factors have risen over time, the minimum wage has adjusted accordingly.

As with any issue there are people in favor of minimum wage laws, and many opposed. Supporters of minimum wage laws believe that it lends a hand to those who do not have the technical skills to get higher paying jobs. Having a higher minimum wage also increases the national average wage. Having a higher minimum wage also gives incentive to some people to seek a job when they otherwise would not. A higher minimum wage also encourages increased efficiency. If an employer must pay workers a certain amount then they will strive to eliminate any unnecessary positions. Additionally workers who receive more pay will be more motivated to work hard.

On the other hand, many of the benefits of minimum wage also inadvertently create problems. For example, the fact that minimum wages entice people to seek jobs that would otherwise chose not to means that there is an increased demand for jobs. However, because minimum wage also encourages efficiency and the elimination of unnecessary position there are fewer jobs available. This creates the appearance that unemployment has actually gone up. Another possible negative effect is that businesses may pass on the cost of paying employees to customers in the form of increased prices on products or services. A higher minimum wage can also become enticing to some and encourage them to enter to work for and get jobs instead of seeking further education.

WARN ACT

The WARN Act is one way that government regulations are used to monitor relations between employees and employers. The Workers Adjustment and Retraining Notification Act (also known as WARN Act) requires that employers give at least 60 days advance warning to employees before a plant closure or mass layoff. This allows the workers to adjust their lives accordingly, such as by seeking other employment or making training arrangements.

CONFIDENTIALITY

Another issue that arises between employees and employers is the idea of confidentiality. Often in the workplace there is information which should or needs to remain private. For example, personal or financial information of customers should remain private. Unless the business has informed the individual that their information will not be kept private, it is the business', and therefore the employee's, responsibility to ensure that it does remain private. As another example, key information relative to the business, like recipes or elements of product design, may be something that the business wishes to keep confidential. In cases such as this it is important that an employee understand what is and isn't necessary to keep confidential and work to ensure that it does remain confidential. In some cases, a company may require that their employees sign a Non-Disclosure Agreement.

A Non-Disclosure Agreement (NDA) is an agreement between two or more groups to keep information private. For example, if a company decides to share sensitive information with a potential investor, they may ask them to sign an NDA stating that they will not disclose the information that they are shown. This sort of agreement extends to situations in which the employer wishes to ensure that the employee does not disclose important information to anyone outside the company (or anyone inside the company that does not need access to the specific information).

Also, if two companies are working together to create a product they may each contribute information to it which they want kept confidential. They may create an NDA to restrict the information that either company may share once the project is complete. Typically NDAs specify the parties which are involved in the NDA, describe the information which must remain confidential, specifies a time period over which the information may be shared and describes obligations of the person receiving the information. Basically, an NDA says who is not allowed to discuss what at certain points in time.

All NDAs have a time specification. This is for a number of reasons. One reason is that in some cases the information will not necessarily remain confidential indefinitely. It could be that a certain technology is developed that a business wishes to have remain confidential. However, within a few years there could be many companies which have developed similar technologies. Were there not a time specification to the NDA the person who had signed it would never be able to discuss the technology, even if it were to become public knowledge. In this way, the time specification becomes a protection and benefit to the individual who must keep information confidential. In another case it could be that the information should in fact remain confidential indefinitely. In a case such as this the NDA would specify that the term of the agreement was indefinite.

NDAs will also state the purpose for which the information is being disclosed. For example, if two companies were working together to produce a piece of software, than the NDA would state that project was the purpose of disclosing the information. This prevents one of the companies from using the information to develop their own line independently of the other company.

WHISTLE BLOWING

The discussion of NDAs brings up another issue related to employer-employee relations: incidences of whistle blowing. A whistleblower is a person who comes forward with information exposing wrongdoing by or within a company. Even in cases when it may seem like the employee is responsible to keep information about their employer's work private, such as if the corruption involves information in an NDA, the employee is legally obligated to expose the corruption. Whistle blowing can occur at many levels, involve many different forms of corruption and have many different eventual results.

For example, whistle blowing could occur on a small scale. If an employee were to discover that another employee was stealing paper, staplers, light bulbs or other sorts of office supplies from the company and then selling it online, then informing their supervisors would be a form of whistle blowing. On the other hand, whistle blowing can occur on a much larger scale, in which case the informant would have to possibly go to authorities to report the problem. For example, if the head accountant at a major firm was creating false contracts to increase the publicly reported net income, it would be the responsibility of anyone who discovered this to inform the manager or even government agencies which are responsible to prosecute those who are discovered committing accounting fraud.

One example of large scale whistle blowing would be the Enron scandal. The accounting fraud and misappropriation of money by the company's executives was exposed by an employee, Sherron Watkins, the Vice President of Corporate Development. Her actions resulted in investigation of the company which revealed the millions of dollars stolen from the company and the arrest of those responsible.

Both of the examples given refer to accounting fraud, but whistle blowing can relate to any activity which an employee believes to be either illegal or unethical. However, in order to protect the rights of the business and protect their privacy, it is important that a person consider whether the issue in question is truly unethical or illegal, and not just a matter of different interpretations of policy or ethical standards between management and employees that could be easily resolved. Examples of reasons for whistle blowing could include violations of health and safety regulations that are meant to protect workers or regulations which are designed to protect the environment, untruthful advertising slogans or campaigns, bribery, discrimination or theft.

There are also many different responses that can occur as a result of whistle blowing. Often those who discover corruption are afraid to come forward with their knowledge out of fear of the consequences that may befall them. In one famous case involving Kerr-McGee, a company which produced plutonium pellets to fuel nuclear reactors, an employee named Karen Silkwood noted that the security measures at the plant were not inadequate and not in line with regulations. She began building a case, but soon died under mysterious circumstances. However, that sort of situation is rare, and in some cases whistleblowers are even promoted to higher positions within a company because of their actions.

There are numerous laws and regulations which are designed to encourage and protect whistleblowers. For example, the Whistleblower Protection Act. This act protects employees of the federal government who expose incidences of waste of funds, abuse of authority, violations of laws or any other issue from any action being taken against them. If an employee feels that they are being retaliated against in some way, then they may file a complaint and have the issue taken care of.

Another protection developed for whistleblowers is the False Claims Act. The False Claims Act works from the opposite end of the Whistleblower Protection Act and encourages employees to expose efforts by companies to avoid paying federal taxes, providing false information to the federal government, conspiring to do either of those things or other acts which involve fraud towards the federal government. The act allows for compensation to the whistleblower of between 15 and 30 percent of the amount recovered as a result of their informing.

A third act with implications for whistleblowers is the Sarbanes-Oxley Act. The act has four elements relating to whistleblowers. The first is that a company must have a system of internal auditing through which an employee can file complaints. The second is that the act creates a legal responsibility for lawyers to inform on clients who are in violation of SEC regulations. The third is that the act prohibited any form of retaliation by employers to employees who legally inform about ethics violations to the proper sources, and provided the whistleblower with compensation for any legal fees. The fourth element of the act is that it allows for violators of any of the other elements can be charged under criminal law.

SEXUAL HARASSMENT

Another ethical issue which often arises in the workplace is the issue of sexual harassment. Sexual harassment is defined as any repeated, unwanted behavior of a sexual nature. This definition extends to both physical actions, words, images and written material. In order for a person to claim sexual harassment, they have to be able to show that the harassment created a hostile work environment.

A hostile work environment is created when an action is unwanted, severe, and it has an effect on the claimant's ability to work. In more detail, that the action must have been unwanted is an important element. Although many actions are unethical in a workplace setting, they are protected under the Constitution in a private, consensual setting. Sexual harassment laws can differ from state to state and in some cases, if it is unclear whether the claimant was offended or affected by the act (if others had a reasonable belief that they did not consider it unacceptable) than it is difficult to prove that it created a hostile work environment.

That the action must have been severe means that it must have been hostile, pervasive or offensive enough that the claimant feels it alters their conditions of employment. For example, if the actions create a work environment which is outside the reasonable expectations of the employee. Another way that sexual harassment can alter the conditions of employment is by forcing them into an unethical dual relationship. A dual relationship occurs when two people who work together or share professional responsibilities are in a relationship with one another. This is not necessarily unethical. However, an unethical dual relationship occurs when that relationship interferes with their professional responsibilities. This can be considered in two ways. If a person is in a consensual relationship with a person that works for them it provides an opportunity for them to advance or benefit the person they are in a relationship with, then it would be unethical for them to do so. Another way of looking at unethical dual relationships is if a person feels that their job is contingent on going along with the relationship. In this way it alters the conditions of employment by forcing them into a relationship. When a person feels that their employment status is dependent on responding to unwelcome sexual advances it is referred to as quid pro quo sexual harassment (**quid pro quo** means "this for that" in Latin).

The final, and most important, factor in determining whether a hostile work environment was created is whether the action had an effect on the claimant's ability to work. To make a sexual harassment case, the claimant does not need to show that it affected their psychological well-being or harmed them in any way, it just has to interfere with their work ability. As a part of this qualification, the action must be shown to be something which a reasonable person would find hostile or offensive. The biggest concern in the case of sexual harassment is not the intent of the act, but its impact.

This standard was established in the case of Harris vs. Forklift Systems, Inc. In this case the court ruled that the claimant Teresa Harris did in fact have a legitimate claim at a sexual harassment case. Her employer had made multiple commends that were degrading to her as a female employee and would make other inappropriate comments about her clothes or other things. Because the comments were things that any "reasonable person" would feel offense at and because she felt that it affected her ability to work, the court ruled in her favor even though it was not damaging psychologically.

There are a number of steps that a business can and should take to ensure that sexual harassment is kept to a minimum. For one, there should be a policy which dictates an individual to be responsible for preventing harassment within the company. The policy should also strictly define sexual harassment and inform employees about acceptable and unacceptable behaviors. It is also important that there are established procedures for employees to report incidences of sexual harassment, and that the complaints are dealt with in an appropriate and timely manner. Most importantly, the policy should be designed to encourage victims to come forward with information, and then protect them from any form of retaliation that could emerge.

DISCRIMINATION

Another important issue which arises between employers and employees is the problem of discrimination. On the most basic level, discrimination is an issue of personal beliefs and ethics. However, when that element of personal ethics is demonstrated in a business setting it does become an issue of business ethics and can often create ethical conflicts within a workplace. Any discrimination which occurs on a basis of race, color, ethnicity (a person's cultural origin), national origin, religion, gender, marital status, disability, public assistance status (if they are receiving financial aid in some form from the government), age or sexual orientation is illegal in the United States.

There are a number of ways that a company could be considered to be in violation of antidiscrimination laws. For example, if a company chose not to hire an individual because of their status in relation to one of the mentioned factors it would be considered discrimination and the company could be sued. However, if a company can provide reasonable justification for not hiring workers that fall into certain categories it may be found legal. For example, if a modeling company is hiring for a new line of female clothing, it would make sense that they would hire only female models. However, it is never allowable to discriminate on a basis of race. The question of whether or not something is discrimination becomes more confusing as questions are raised relating, for example, to whether or not religious schools should be allowed, to hire only teachers that are members of a specific church, or if they can fire a teacher after teaching with standards and views that were not in line with what the leaders of the school believed. Another issue is if employers should be allowed to set age limitations after which an employee must retire.

Another way that a company could be considered to be discriminating is if, rather than having a policy of just not hiring people in a certain category, they create a situation which favors certain types of people to an unreasonable extent or excludes certain people to an unreasonable extent. For example, requiring applicants to have a PhD to apply for a position would exclude any person in their early twenties because they will not have had the time to go through the necessary schooling. However, because it relates to job qualifications the "discrimination" against people of that age is not considered unreasonable and is therefore not discrimination. On the other hand, if an employer were to create a program which unreasonably leaned hiring practices in favor of males under the age of thirty that were single and born in the United States than the practice would clearly be discriminatory.

Discrimination that occurs naturally on a basis of job qualifications is referred to as unintentional discrimination or statistical discrimination. This refers to the fact that a business may statistically have a disproportionate number of workers that fall into a certain category, but it doesn't necessarily mean that they are doing so deliberately or carelessly. For example, there may be a higher average wage for men that women in the United States, however it is also true that women are more likely to work for non-profit organizations or other naturally lower paying jobs. Another example would be if it appeared that a company had a higher than normal proportion of Asian workers, but when accounting for educational differences among employees and applicants the appearance of discrimination is proved to be invalid. Situations such as this where there is unintentional discrimination or statistical discrimination are not considered to be illegal.

A third way that discrimination could occur within a workplace is in firing practices. For example, if the economy were to take a downturn and a company were forced to lay off a large portion of its employees and they chose to fire only (or first) those that were disabled, or female, or born outside of the United States or Atheist it would be considered discriminatory. However, if the company fired employees on a basis of the last employee hired was the first that they fired, or those with the lowest quality reviews or those that went to the littlest amount of college first it would not be considered discriminatory because the system wouldn't inherently favor firing a person on a basis of any of the factors that are considered illegal discrimination.

Another way a company could discriminate is if they were to consider any of the factors and unfairly penalize a person because of them in employment terms. For example, pay, health care programs, pay raises, hours or other factors. This means that it is illegal for a company to discriminate by categorically paying some employees less on a basis of one of those factors, or giving promotions to only people in certain groups.

One example of this is the case of **Dukes vs. Wal-Mart.** In this case, Betty Dukes attempted to sue Wal-Mart on behalf of all of its female employees because she believed that men were unfairly promoted above women, and were given more training opportunities that allowed for advancement. Though she initially won the suit, the Supreme Court ruled in favor of Wal-Mart because Dukes could not prove that all women employees of Wal-Mart faced discriminatory practices.

In another case, **Watson vs. Fort Worth Bank and Trust,** the bank's employee, Clara Watson, sued after being passed over four times for promotions which were given instead to white applicants. Watson believed that the bank's hiring system, which relied only on the impressions of the supervisors, was inherently discriminatory although there was no outright system of discrimination. The court ruled that Watson did in fact have a right to sue, but they dismissed her case because she could not produce sufficient statistical evidence to prove that she was a victim of discrimination. The result of the case was, therefore, that employers could legally use any combination of subjective and objective considerations in hiring employees as long as they did not have an adverse or discriminatory effect.

Finally, a business could also be accused of discrimination if it were to discriminate against groups of customers. For example, a recent complaint that has arisen is discrimination by airlines against passengers from Middle Eastern countries. Although airlines deny that they are not in violation of any discrimination laws, many have spent millions of dollars training employees to be sensitive to possible civil rights violations of passengers.

Tens of thousands of discrimination complaints are filed every year which relate to race, gender and age discrimination. These complaints are addressed by the **Equal Employment Opportunity Commission (EEOC).** In economic terms, any form of employment discrimination could be said to create a "glass ceiling" to the progress of a group. A glass ceiling is described as an invisible barrier to the advancement of a group. For example, if with copious equality laws, statistics show that the average female worker in the United States still earns only a fraction of what the average male worker makes. Some people argue that this is a result of an irrational glass ceiling that female workers must face. Affirmative action programs and comparative worth movements are both attempts to eliminate the glass ceilings which are hindering the progress of involved groups. Because affirmative action programs often face public criticisms (many people accuse them of creating reverse-discrimination) the Supreme Court has set forth guidelines for creating affirmative action programs.

One guideline is that there must be a strong, and demonstrable, reason for initiating an affirmative action program. This means that if a person cannot definitively prove that discrimination exists then a program which aimed at helping certain groups of people would be unethical and could not be legally instituted. This would be a situation in which the program actually created reverse discrimination. Rather than benefitting historically harmed or disadvantaged groups it would merely promote the good of one group above the others.

Another guideline is that the program should apply only to qualified candidates. For example, a program meant to benefit Hispanics should not, by design, disproportionately benefit Hispanic women or Hispanic men. This goes back to the requirement to demonstrate a reason for initiating the program. If, even within an otherwise acceptable program, there is a second group being benefitted that was not considered to be benefitted before, than the program is unfit and should be revised.

The third guideline is that affirmative action programs cannot be permanently and rigidly defined. For example, in multiple cases the Supreme Court has ruled that it is illegal for an institution to create affirmative action programs that create quota systems. The programs should be designed to be temporary, so that the disadvantaged group is quickly moved to a position of fairness and then things are returned to a normal, competitive state.

UNIONS AND LABOR RELATIONS

The final issue of employer-employee relations which will be discussed is management relations with labor unions. The employees of every workplace have the right to form a union if that is their desire. Stated most simply, labor unions are legal entities with the ability to bargain on behalf of workers to improve working conditions. When at least 30% of a company's workers verbally state a desire for union representation, a secret ballot is taken to determine if a majority of the workers wish for one. If a majority vote in favor of union representation then the workers could continue and gain union certification, however if not then at least one year must go by before a vote can be taken again.

Labor unions operate on a basis of collective bargaining. This is the idea that if all of the workers act as one in negotiating with management, than they will have more power in the negotiations than if a single worker were to attempt to negotiate with management. Labor unions deal with issues ranging from workplace safety to wages to how many hours members can be required or allowed to work.

Traditionally there have been many clashes between employers and labor unions as the two groups battle for the upper hand in negotiation. As a result some regulations have been created to avoid unethical practices in management dealing with labor unions. There are certain responsibilities that employers must consider in dealing with labor unions.

A major piece of legislation which relates to management response to labor unions is the Fair Labor Standards Act (FLSA). This act outlines actions that are not allowed by management in an attempt to protect the right of employees to form a union. When an employer violates the Fair Labor Standards Act they can be charged with practicing unfair labor practices. In a general sense the act describes any practices which interfere with the workers ability to create or operate within a union. Some of the specific practices prohibited by the act include interfering with employees attempt to form a union, such as by attempting to coerce them into voting against one, discriminating (such as in hiring and firing practices) against employees that belong to unions or outright refusing to bargain with the unions.

Employers are also responsibilities to negotiate with labor unions. Although they don't have to accept or agree to all proposals by unions, employers are expected to meet and discuss issues with union representatives, bargain in good faith and to address certain subjects. The initial description of required discussion points included wages, hours and employment conditions.

This description has expanded over time to include wages and benefits, grievance procedures, health and safety, discrimination issues, no-strike clauses, the extent of management rights and disciplinary practices. In addition, as part of bargaining in good faith, it is required that the management provides the union with any information that it might need to successfully carry out its duties. This can include the company's financial information and employee records.

EMPLOYEE POLYGRAPH PROTECTION ACT - EPPA

The Employee Polygraph Protection Act of 1988 (EPPA) generally prevents employers from using lie detector tests, either for pre-employment screening or during the course of employment, with certain exemptions.

A polygraph is only one type of lie detector test.

A lie detector includes a polygraph, deceptograph, voice stress analyzer, psychological stress evaluator or similar device (mechanical or electrical) used to determine a diagnostic opinion as to the honesty or dishonesty of an individual.

A polygraph refers to an instrument that records continuously, visually, and simultaneously changes in cardiovascular, respiratory and electrodermal patterns as minimum instrumentation standards and is used create a diagnostic opinion as to the veracity of an individual's statements.

Employers may not require that applicants or employees take a lie detector test, or discharge, discipline, or discriminate against a job applicant or employee for refusing to take a test or for exercising other rights under the Act.

However, there are some significant exceptions.

Federal, state and local governments are excluded. In addition, lie detector tests administered by the Federal Government to employees of Federal contractors engaged in national security intelligence or counterintelligence functions are exempt. The Act also includes limited exemptions where polygraph tests (but no other lie detector tests) may be administered in the private sector, subject to certain restrictions:

- To employees who are reasonably suspected of involvement in a workplace incident that results in economic loss to the employer and who had access to the property that is the subject of an investigation; and

- To prospective employees of armored car, security alarm, and security guard firms who protect facilities, materials or operations affecting health or safety, national security, or currency and other like instruments; and

- To prospective employees of pharmaceutical and other firms authorized to manufacture, distribute, or dispense controlled substances who will have direct access to such controlled substances, as well as current employee who had access to persons or property that are the subject of an ongoing investigation.

Corporations and Stakeholders

The relationship of a corporation to its stakeholders is one of the most fundamental relationships in business ethics. Recall that a stakeholder is any person that is affected by the company, including employees, managers, community members, stockholders and others. Because stakeholders are integrally tied to the corporations success – community members buy products and can influence laws and regulations applied to the corporation, and managers and employees are involved in the day to day operations of the company – it is effectively the stakeholders that decide whether or not something is an ethical issue, or whether or not a company is behaving ethically in any given situation.

Each set of stakeholders involves its own unique set of concerns that the corporation must consider. For example, in some cases problems can arise because stakeholders such as managers or employees may wish to pursue their own interests to the detriment of the company (such as if some sort of conflict of interest were to arise). Because of this problem it is important that companies have set methods of monitoring and controlling employees to ensure that problems such as this do not arise. On the other hand, if a company is considering its customers and members of the community in general they will need to focus more on how they are being portrayed and perceived than on other factors.

As a result of possible conflicts of interest for employees, or any other possible ethical issues which could arise, it is important that companies find a way to prevent employees from making unethical decisions. The manner in which this is accomplished is referred to as corporate governance. Corporate governance is a system of accountability, oversight and control within the company.

Accountability refers to ensuring that workplace decisions are aligned with the ethical principles and goals of the company. The idea behind accountability is to ensure that the employees understand that the company considers ethical conduct to be of importance and that they know and understand the standards that they are expected to adhere to. For example, it could involve simply creating and distributing a company-wide ethical code to employees or having training sessions about how to handle ethical issues.

Oversight refers to a system of checks and balances that restricts the ability of a single person to make an unethical decision. There are essentially three different conditions which have to be met for an employee to act unethically: perceived pressure, rationalization and perceived opportunity. If any one of these factors is removed from the equation an employee will not be able to act unethically. For example, if a person sees an opportunity to act unethically but can think of no reason to do so (i.e., they have no perceived pressure) then they will be honest. If the employee does have pressure and an opportunity to act unethically, but cannot convince themselves that it's acceptable (i.e., they cannot rationalize it) then they will also not act unethically.

However, companies cannot control either the outside pressures that their employees feel or their ability to rationalize. This is where the oversight portion of corporate governance comes in. The point of oversight is to ensure that there is no perceived opportunity for an employee to act unethically (because even if they can rationalize the behavior and have outside pressures to do so, they will not be able to). For example, if a company has a policy that dictates that any handling of cash must involve two or more employees it would be a form of oversight. Another example would be if a company had a policy that all financial calculations made by an accountant would be double checked by another independent employee. In both cases the policy seriously restricts the employee's ability to act unethically.

Finally, the control portion of corporate governance describes evaluation processes which allow the company to consider decisions and improve where necessary. In other words, in the control phase a company will determine whether or not their policies are effective in reducing or subduing ethics violations by employees. If not then they will consider additional policies or determine the sources of the ethics violations to correct any problems.

There are two general models used in considering corporate governance: the shareholder model and the stakeholder model. The shareholder model focuses on maintaining the accountability of directors and officers to the shareholders. In other words, the main focus of this model is the directors and officers acting to best increase benefits to shareholders. Under this model a person would consider the different ways to use the elements of corporate governance (accountability, oversight and control) to ensure that the corporate officers were focused on raising stock prices.

For example, if the shareholder model were being used the company may set up ways of reminding corporate officers of their duty to the shareholders, such as by requiring that they personally give yearly reports to shareholders. Another way of ensuring accountability is by granting high level employees such as boards of directors and corporate officers stock in the company so that they themselves have a stake in stock prices. A program of oversight that they might implement could include hiring multiple officers that would have to approve each other's decisions so that no one officer could act in a way that would be harmful to the company. Periodic evaluations of the company's ethics would be a way to implement the control aspect as it would aid in identifying areas that may need improvement.

Because it is so focused on purely the financial success of the company, the shareholder model is often not considered the best way for a company to operate. The shareholder model is actually considered to be the precursor to the stakeholder model. This model takes a more holistic approach to the company's success. The stakeholder model recognizes the need for considering the shareholders, but acknowledges the accountability to stakeholders as well. Because the way that outsiders to the company perceive the company can affect sales and other measures of success, the stakeholder model can be a more effective method of regulating the company's actions.

Under the stakeholder model of corporate governance, a manager must consider which group of stakeholders is most important to please (consumers, special interest groups, suppliers, etc.), and then work towards developing positive long term relationships with that group. Therefore it would be important that the company have a set of regulations that will monitor that the needs of that group are truly being considered. Of course, this doesn't mean that other groups are neglected or ignored. Rather, it means that the company believes that the particular group of stakeholders will have the greatest effect on the long term success of the company, and hopefully by considering their needs first, all other groups will be benefitted in the long run.

For example, a manufacturing company that operates a large, pollution-producing factory may determine that it is most important that they focus on relations with consumers. It could be that the factory has a large risk of upsetting consumers with its pollution which would be damaging to the business, and this problem would be their focus. On the other hand, the company would have very little gain from focusing their efforts on employees or managers. While there may be small ways in which they could affect the company's success, if it is a manufacturing company where most of the work is machinery based there is likely little that employees can do that would be as devastating to the company as if the consumers were to decide that the company was unethical and should be shut down.

For a different company, however, it may be that the company is most focused on keeping its employees happy. This may be the case with a software designing company. In a case such as this there is little worry that consumers will find the company to be unethical in nature. The only concern would be creating a product that consumers will buy, which falls on the employees. If this company were to behave like the large factory, they would expend resources strengthening relations with consumers and possibly miss out on the opportunity to ensure that their employees were happy. If the employees were unhappy they may choose to relocate to a different company, or be less productive and effective at their jobs than they could be. This could push back release dates or leave the company without new and innovative ideas for future production. Therefore in this case it is clearly more important that a company consider employees their most important group of stakeholders.

In case of either the factory or the software company, there would need to be a method of corporate governance that ensured that the needs of the specific stakeholders were being met. In many cases this can be accomplished in similar ways as would they would be in the shareholder model of corporate governance, but the stakeholder model builds on it by forcing the company to look past just the flat numbers and into what factors really influence the success of the company and could possibly be improved.

This isn't to say that shareholders are unimportant in considering how a company is run. Although they do not have control over day to day operations, shareholders vote on matters relating to the business and can be very influential in putting pressure on managers and boards of directors to act as ethically and responsibly as possible. When shareholders do use their position to influence those running the company it is called shareholder activism. Recently shareholder activism has increased as shareholders have become more interested in knowing the ways in which executives are compensated. Shareholders have also demanded increased transparency and corporate governance, likely as a response to the many corporate scandals in the past few decades.

In both the shareholder and stakeholder model, the leaders of a company play a large role, and it is important that the role of the leaders of an organization not be forgotten.

Managers, corporate officers, boards of directors and others play a large part in developing the ethical culture of a business. When leaders are not acting ethically it reflects badly on the company, and if they are found out it can be very bad for them. For example, if people find out that a CEO has been embezzling money from an organization, that CEO is likely to be fired, and could be sued by the shareholders. Therefore, it is important that leaders show that they are committed to a good ethics program.

They can show this in a number of ways. For example, they could hire outside entities to do evaluations of the ethical practices within the business. The valuable information gathered here could be used to determine what ethical concerns need to be addressed, and determine the opinion of employees about the practices of their coworkers and supervisors. They can also show this by creating and publishing a company-wide ethics policy that outlined how questionable situations should be handled, and the proper method of addressing ethical concerns that do arise. Such policies should be clearly enforced and evaluations should occur periodically so that employees view the commitment as legitimate and so that new information can be gathered to determine the effectiveness.

Besides simply showing support for ethical programs, it is important that leaders shown that they themselves demonstrate a commitment to ethical actions and values within the company. Style of leadership can also be an important component of both the extent to which a leader is considered ethical and whether or not the employees will chose to adhere to ethical standards that they set forth. A leadership style that is conductive to a strong ethical culture can influence the extent to which employees accept the norms, values and codes of ethics. It can also affect how they will interact with each other.

Understanding the leadership style in a company is also a good way to determine where future ethical issues may arise. If the leader does not effectively promote ethical habits, it can be a sign that ethics will not be very firmly set. Employees typically look to their leaders in determining how to act in a situation, even if they already know that it is unethical or illegal. The concept of ethical leadership extends not only to the boards of directors, CEOs and senior managers of a company, but also to lower level managers, supervisors and even employees. Cultivating a strong ethical support for the company at all of these levels ensures, in turn, that a strong ethical culture will develop which will be a benefit to the company in the long run.

Because ethics can in many cases come down to a matter of opinion and personal values, it is essentially impossible that a leader will be considered ethical in every decision that they ever make. The sheer number of unique situations that could arise make it so that determining the most ethical course can be difficult. To be the most effective a leader should be able to tailor their style of leadership as the situation demands. For example, knowing when to push employees and when to be friendly and create a collaborative environment. Or, being able to see when it is necessary to create an open, trusting and friendship oriented environment as opposed to when to set a schedule and ensure that expectations are met. An ethical leader should have the strong moral character and sufficient experience to be an example of ethics to those around them.

LEADERSHIP STYLES

There are three basic types of leaders: authoritative, democratic and free reign. Authoritative leadership is also often referred to as autocratic leadership. This type of leader is very concerned with the power structure. They decide what needs to be done and tell employees what they are to do. The style doesn't allow for much communication or sharing of opinions, but if time is short or there are other extenuating circumstances it can be the most appropriate form for a leader to adopt. It can also be the most effective style if there is a large number of workers and collecting individual input is not really feasible. However, if there isn't a huge time crunch and the leader wishes to cultivate a more open environment and get multiple perspectives, the democratic leadership style would be preferred to the authoritative style.

The democratic leadership style can also be referred to as the participative leadership style. This is because it involves a joint effort between employers or supervisors and employees. Rather than simply making decisions on their own, the leader would collaborate with the employees to determine the most effective path to take. This style can be extremely useful if, for example, a specialized task must be performed and the leader doesn't have all of the information necessary to make the decision. In this case it would be necessary that they receive input from the employees about various factors relating to the project.

The third leadership style, free reign, can also be referred to as laissez-faire or delegative leadership. In this style the leader delegates responsibilities to the workers and allows them to make decisions. This style can be the most effective if the workers are all highly skilled, responsible and capable workers. It requires that the leaders have trust in their employee's abilities. However, if this system of leadership develops because a leader does not effectively take control and doesn't take interest in the employee than it can be very detrimental to productivity in the workplace, and it would need to be addressed.

Another way that leadership styles can be classified is as either transactional or transformational. Transactional leaders work to create a system of rewards and punishments within a workplace. They ensure that things get done by offering rewards or punishments on a basis of the efforts and successes of the employees. For example, if a supervisor were to offer a pay raise to an employee if they finished a certain project ahead of schedule it would be an example of transactional leadership. The supervisor set the goal and reward and the employee works to meet it. On the other hand, if an employee is chronically late or misses work without explanation, they will most likely be fired. This too is an example of transactional leadership. The employee failed to meet expectations and was punished. Basically employers and employees relate to each other on a basis of bartering for desired behaviors or rewards.

One of the benefits of the style is that it can be considered to be motivational in the sense that it allows employees to obtain a clear picture of what is expected of them, and the benefits of doing their job well. It is also a very stable way to ensure that all expectations are met, and that values and norms are observed by employees. However, there are a number of criticisms of the style as well. For example, the leader's position is solely reliant on their ability to furnish rewards or enforce punishments. Also, the transactional style is, of necessity, focused in the short term. Goals and incentives are set on a basis of current problems and issues. The employees have no reason to look beyond these short term expectations. Some people also consider this style to be too authoritative and control oriented to be an effective model of leadership.

A transformational leader worries less about incentive and punishment systems and more about creating a culture of progress and improvement for employees. They focus on raising the levels of commitment and motivation of their employees to improve their overall productivity and usefulness to the company as a whole. Transformational leaders want to help their employees derive a sense of pride, enjoyment and accomplishment from their work. Because their focus is on improving the employee and helping them to become more productive, transformational leaders are more likely than transactional leaders to consider the employees needs or problems that they may be facing.

There are many benefits that arise from a transformational leadership style. For example, because leaders show an interest in their employees the employees develop a loyalty to both their leader and the company. This is useful when the company goes through down times or has other problems. The transformational style of leadership is more likely to generate an awareness of and respect for ethical principles within a workplace.

The difference between the transactional and transformational leadership has been described as transactional leaders work within the existing ethical framework of the company, whereas transformational leaders try to change and improve the ethical culture. Neither transformational nor transactional leadership is considered to be outright better than the alternative, and most people believe that a truly effective leader should be able to use both styles as the situation may demand.

CODES OF ETHICS

In addition to the leadership style, a company's code of ethics can affect the way that employees act as well. No matter what they say specifically, the basic point of a code of ethics is to provide a certain amount of predictability in how employees will respond to situations. There are two different types of codes of ethics: compliance oriented and value oriented.

A compliance oriented ethics program is based on a set of standards that employees must agree to abide by, and a set of punishments for violating those behaviors. For example, most schools give students a disciplinary pathway that will be followed if they disobey rules, such as with first violation is a verbal warning, second violation they get sent to the principal's office and the third time their parents will be called and so forth. This would be an example of a compliance oriented program. In a business setting the program may involve steps such as probationary status or, eventually, that they will be fired. These sorts of programs involve extensive definition of terms and legal language because standards of ethics are specifically laid out for the employees. The employees would also have to be taught, either in seminars or through distribution of hard copies of the information, the set of standards that they would have to adhere to, and how to react to certain situations.

A values oriented program, on the other hand, is less formally laid out. It would still set forth some standards and punishments for obvious ethical violations, but instead of going into great detail about specific actions they focus more on ensuring that employees adhere to a set of core values. The system is based on abstractions such as respect or honesty or integrity.

The two programs have both shown to be beneficial to the workplace. In the short run, both types of programs will enhance awareness of employees about ethical issues, and increase their ability to respond to such problems in a satisfactory manner. However, in the long run, values oriented programs are typically preferable. It increases the belief among employees that they are operating in an ethics oriented workplace, and increases the level of open communication both with coworkers and superiors.

Although the style of leadership that an employer practices can have a great influence in relations with employees, sometimes it is also necessary for there to be some sort of intermediary in a workplace. This person could be referred to as an ombudsman. An ombudsman is a person who is hired by a group (it could be the managers or a business or even the government) to look into complaints that are filed against it. Having an ombudsman can help the workplace operate more efficiently because it allows employees a method through which to voice problems which are occurring.

 Ethics in International Business

Various advancements in transportation and communication have made large scale trade increasingly common and feasible. Widespread use of the internet allows trades to occur in seconds between people on opposite sides of the globe who have never met or talked to one another. Advancements in travel also allow goods to be shipped around the world with increasing ease. More and more companies are finding themselves able to move into a global market.

INTERNATIONAL ORGANIZATIONS

When it comes to discussing ethical business practices on an international sphere, a number of concerns are raised. The biggest problem is that there is as yet no universal, enforced ethical code which businesses in different countries can reference. Organizations such as the World Trade Organization (WTO), North American Free Trade Agreement (NAFTA) and European Union have attempted to create a standardized set of business ethics, but have as of yet been largely unsuccessful.

Not only do each of these organizations work to create a universalized ethics standard, but also to create conformities in other matters as well. The World Bank and the International Monetary Fund (IMF) are two international organizations which were simultaneously created in 1944. The IMF is an organization which has the responsibility of stabilizing international trade, and preventing international trade crises. It regulates the trade deficits of countries, and can loan them money if it is necessary. However, the IMF loans money on conditions of it being used to generate a surplus of products traded internationally. The IMF ideology is that a country will be able to repay loans because they have healthy economies.

On the other hand, the World Bank has the responsibility of fostering economic development. It also loans money to countries, but with the purpose of the countries using that money to grow economically. Therefore, the money can be used, for example, to strengthen infrastructure, schools or hospitals. The World Bank ideology is that by loaning developing countries money they will be able to repay it when their economy grows.

NAFTA and the WTO are both organizations created to deal with international trade, however they are two distinct entities with different goals. The North American Free Trade Agreement (NAFTA) is an agreement signed between Canada, Mexico and the United States. The primary purpose of NAFTA is to lower trading barriers and dealing with trade disputes between the three countries. It is governed by three Secretariats (one in each country).

The World Trade Organization (WTO) deals with trade on a global level. It is governed via a Ministerial conference held every two years and which appoints a director general to oversee day to day organization. The goal of the WTO is to eliminate barriers to trade, help developing countries in trade matters, supervise international trade and settle trade disputes among member countries.

Non-governmental organizations have also formed such as the Caux Round Table. The Caux Round Table is a Swiss organization which works to create awareness in businesses around the globe and teach tools and strategies to maintain a minimum ethical standard. However, despite the efforts of these many groups, the diversity of the world's economies and cultures has made it very difficult to create a standard that everyone is comfortable with. In many cases there are values which are considered important in any culture, such as the generic "truth" and "virtue." The real problem is that the application of these values differs across cultures.

One case in which an individual industry has been able to create some ethical standards is with the Kimberley Process Certification Scheme. The Kimberley Process Certification Scheme (KPCS) was created in 2003 to stop the circulation of conflict diamonds (which are also called blood diamonds or war diamonds). Conflict diamonds are diamonds which are mined and sold by countries or groups in order to fund insurrection or war. The KPCS states that rough diamonds (uncut diamonds) must be shipped in tamper proof containers and be certified.

CULTURAL ETHICS

The fact that different ethical standards exist between countries creates a perceived "us" and "them" status in discussing ethics. Businesspeople traveling to foreign countries and doing business in foreign countries will tend to see the laws and standards in other countries ("them") through a filter of comparison to their origin country ("us"). In some cases this may create a sense of superiority when the person is from a country with high ethical standards. On the other hand, there are also cases where businesses transition into countries with high ethical standards. For example, some of the countries which are perceived to have the most ethical business standards include Iceland, Denmark, Australia, the United Kingdoms, Germany and the United States. On the other hand, Bangladesh, Haiti, Ethiopia, Rwanda, India and Pakistan are some examples of countries which are perceived to have the least ethical business standards. This way of considering ethical standards in relative terms is referred to as the self-reference criterion.

The self-reference criterion is an unconscious method of judgment. A person's perceptions of the world emerge from their past experiences and their values. These tend to be highly influenced by the culture in which a person is raised. Because of this, their culture becomes their standard point of reference in considering ethical situations. Culture is also a very important factor in considering all aspects of business, whether ethical issues are raised or not.

The simplest way to define culture is that it is anything in a person's environment which is related to dealing with or was created by people. Culture can include language, food, customs, societal expectations, architecture and many other aspects. The unique nature of cultures is a large part of why it is very difficult to create worldwide standards. Even innocent and simple gestures can be misunderstood or misconstrued when dealing with different cultures. In the United States, for example, a person nods their head to signify agreement with what is being said. However, in Albania the opposite is true. Going further, for a British person a nod indicates merely that they are listening and does not imply that they agree or disagree with you.

That particular culture difference would be a result of differing interpretations of body language. (Body language describes the way that people's bodies are used in communication, such as through gestures, poses or facial expressions.) The importance of body language can also come into play in many other ways. For example, the distance at which people stand when communicating can often create uncomfortable situations. In the United States and most Western European countries the comfortable standing distance is farther apart, whereas with Japanese or South American cultures it is closer together. In some cultures bowing is an important sign of respect and should be reciprocated appropriately. Clearly body language can be an important element of successful business interaction that can cause difficulties if people do not take the time to understand the culture which they will be operating in.

Actual language can also be a cultural barrier to international business. A statement which is lost in translation, or words that have different or illogical meanings in other languages, can create confusion or result in negative reactions to a person or product. For example, while "china" translates as orange in Puerto Rico, it translates as baboon in Cuba and refers to a type of ceramic material or the actual country in other places. The way that people in different markets perceive the name of a product can have a great effect on its success or failure.

Communication styles can also be a notable factor. Business meetings in the United States tend to be viewed as aggressive by people of other cultures. This is because American businesspeople place a high importance on effective communication and finding the best options. They will debate and argue different points. It is typically accepted that the differences in opinions are not personal attacks. However, other cultures may view this as personal confrontation.

Even simple perceptions of time can be a hindrance to effective business dealings. While punctuality is valued in the United States, other countries appreciate a relaxed and more drawn out approach to business meetings that can be frustrating to American firms. Religious differences can also create problems. For example, a fast food restaurant that sells hamburgers would likely face protests and extreme criticism in India where the dominant religion is Hinduism and the consumption of beef products in considered morally unacceptable.

An interesting question that comes to mind in considering different cultural standards is deciding what cultural norms should be adhered to. Should a company that demands punctuality override a company that likes to take their time, or should the company that demands punctuality accept that there is a cultural difference? Although questions addressing purely cultural factors are important and should be addressed by a business, often the question of more concern relates to the ethical standards. Or in other words, should a company doing business in a country with lower ethical standards remain true to the standards in their origin country or conform to those that they are facing in the current area? Adhering to less ethical practices based on location (as opposed to maintaining the same practices regardless of location) is referred to as cultural relativism.

Global companies face unique exposure to the difficulties that arise in creating an ethical code. For example, Wal-Mart has many stores in the United States. Because they have operations in the United States it is generally expected that they should have a stated code of ethics which sets forth ethical guidelines for their employees. However, although the ethical standards may adhere perfectly to United States laws, it could easily violate laws in other countries in which there are operations. For example, protections for whistleblowers are standard in the United States, but violate privacy laws in other countries. Another factor could be if minimum wage laws varied from country to country.

There are a number of steps that a global company can follow in helping to create a code of ethics. Firstly, the code should be written by a board of individuals with members representative of all nations in which the company operates. This way it is less likely that cultural conflicts will be overlooked in its development. Second, the company needs to be sure that it can enforce the standards that it creates by considering possible legal restrictions or conflicts. Third, the company should be sure that it pays particular attention to any graphics that it publishes. Color can be a powerful tool, but when not used properly it could also create problems. Not only does the company need to be sensitive to include various applicable races in any pictures that it produces, but they should also be cautious in their use of symbols and colors which can take on different meanings in different cultures. Finally, the company should test the program with various smaller groups and translate it into any necessary languages.

Although it's true that there is no universally accepted and enforced ethical code, there are a number of standards of significance. One is the Global Sullivan Principles. The original Sullivan Principles were created by a Reverend Leon Sullivan as an attempt to break down break down racism in South Africa, after twenty years he amended them and applied them to a worldwide audience as the Global Sullivan Principles (GSP). Principles of the GSP include promoting equal opportunity for all races, promoting respect for human rights, respect of intellectual property (copyrights, trademarks and trade secrets), refusing to accept bribes, and ensuring employee safety. The GSP has been accepted by over 30 large companies. However, this is all voluntary and is not enforced by any governing body.

Another important standard which was agreed to by over fifty of the world's largest companies is the United Nations' Global Compact. The Global Compact focuses on protecting the environment, abolishing child labor and permitting unions to form. The companies that accept it are required to give updates on their status with relation to the standards. They are also expected to respect UN policies that apply in any countries that they operate in.

An important attempt at universal ethics is the Kyoto Protocol, which applies specifically to environmental issues. The Kyoto Protocol is an amendment to the United Nations Framework Convention on Climate Change (UNFCCC) and is so named because it was negotiated in Kyoto, Japan. The protocol is a legally binding agreement which aims at reducing the collective worldwide greenhouse gas emissions by 5.2% (assigning individual reduction levels to different countries) as compared to the year 1990. A majority of industrialized nations support the Kyoto Protocol, with the notable exceptions of the United States and Australia.

MULTINATIONAL/TRANSNATIONAL CORPORATIONS

The concept of international ethics is especially relevant in discussing multinational corporations (MNC). An MNC is a company which is publicly traded (i.e. a person could buy stock in the company) and which has a strong enough presence in multiple countries that it does not identify with any single country. MNCs have great potential to influence worldwide policy. It has been known to happen that an MNC even generates more in revenue than the Gross Domestic Product of some countries. The ethical concerns which face MNCs are often similar to those that face regular companies, but on a wider scale. Some specific examples being: discrimination, bribery, and human rights issues.

In the 1970's it was discovered that many U.S. companies operating in foreign countries were paying large bribes (totaling over $300 million) to high government officials to ensure that preferential treatment and business was given to their companies. Of course, these companies were not alone in the practice of bribery. In countries around the world bribery is a normal part of business and a common practice. However, in 1977 the Foreign Corrupt Practices Act was passed, making it illegal for any United States citizen to bribe a foreign official. It also made it illegal for anyone (citizen or not) on U.S. soil to further such payments.

Within the United States, the policy is useful for decreasing corruption in business, but it can be a great disadvantage to international businesses because bribery is not illegal in other countries. Therefore, if an American business were to compete with a business from another country to contract on a job, the other country would be able to bribe officials to get the contract where the American business would not. This technically puts American firms at a disadvantage to all other firms in a global sense.

The Foreign Corrupt Practices Act does, however, have an interesting exception in it. The act actually allows the use of what are called grease payments. When a person pays a low level official of a foreign country to make something happen faster than it normally would, then it is called a grease payment or facilitating payment. In some ways a grease payment may seem very similar to a bribe, however because of some specific distinctions it was decided that they would not be classified as such and are not prosecuted under the act.

BRIBE OR GREASE PAYMENT?

There are two main distinctions which are used to determine whether a payment is counted as a bribe or a grease payment. Firstly, grease payments involve relatively small amounts of money. For example, it is estimated that bribery in the world today is in the hundreds of billions of dollars. While grease payments may involve large amounts of money in a general sense, such as tens of thousands of dollars, in comparison they are fairly small. The second, and more important, factor in defining a grease payment is that they involve an attempt to make an official do their job faster. Bribes, on the other hand, attempt to influence someone to make a decision that they wouldn't normally make. MNCs may use grease payments to avoid long waits for work visas, permits or customs clearance. In this way they can make themselves more competitive (or at least less disadvantaged) in overseas markets.

A common example of a grease payment could be a UPS store. If a person pays a slightly higher price, they can have their mail classified as a priority and it will arrive at its intended destination faster than it would otherwise. Although it isn't necessarily on the same scale as a grease payment by an MNC would be, it is still technically a grease payment. There is nothing illegal about attempting to get a package delivered faster. However, if instead a person were to pay an employee of UPS an extra amount of money to convince them to overlook a shipment of illegal drugs or weapons, then it would be a bribe. In this case, the person is trying to convince the UPS employee to do something that they normally wouldn't allow. Another example could be people paying to expedite their passports. It is legal to pay for the application to be processed faster and it would be considered a grease payment. But if a person paid an official to approve them for a passport when they don't qualify for one, then it would be illegal and a bribe.

Bribery can also take many other forms outside of monetary compensation. A bribe can also exist in the form of promotions, tips, special consideration, stock options, or any form of property. Gift giving can also be a very ethically questionable practice. Gifts can easily be seen as a form of bribery because giving a gift involves the transfer of physical property of value. However, gift giving can also be a considerate way of showing gratitude or respect between businesspeople. In many areas of the world it is expected that gifts will be given during negotiations. For example, in India gift giving is a widespread practice. However, in other areas of the world such as Singapore gift giving is a shunned practice (it is seen as a sign of corruption) and a businessperson would most likely be offended if offered a gift.

CULTURAL DISCRIMINATION

Discrimination is also a bigger problem on a worldwide scale, simply because every culture has a different approach to discrimination. Although in the United States most forms of discrimination is illegal, the practice is still prevalent throughout the world. For example, the prevalence of the Hindu caste system in India often results in discrimination. Also, often in places in Africa and Australia people from aboriginal tribes are discriminated against in urban areas. A third common example is discrimination against females in business in Middle Eastern countries. Whether or not a business actually practices discrimination, they are still influenced by its effects.

For example, if an American company was negotiating with a Middle Eastern company and they sent a female representative then the chances are that the Middle Eastern representatives would either refuse to or be upset about having to negotiate with her. The American company would therefore need to consider whether they would be careful to send only male representatives to ensure that negotiations go more smoothly and favorably, or whether they send female representatives anyways so that they cannot be accused of discriminating against their female employees.

International corporations are also often scrutinized for the possibility of any human rights violations. Especially in the United States, consumers are likely to be critical of and show disdain if they discover that a company is unethical in their practices. Human rights violations can include things such as sweat shop like working conditions in foreign factories, wages below subsistence levels, discrimination or the use of child labor.

The Human Rights Watch is a global organization which works to expose and reduce incidences of human rights violations. They set forth three guidelines that managers and executives should consider as it relates to protecting human rights. First, they believe that communication between management and employees is critical. They advocate open and clear lines of communication.

Second, they encourage managers to be informed about the issues that are specific to the region in which they are operating. Because cultures around the world face different standards it is important that managers do not inadvertently ignore any human rights issues. Information about human rights issues can be found through Amnesty international, another nonprofit organization which works to end human rights abuses.

Finally, while the Human Rights Watch does believe companies need to meet the minimum legal requirements as far as human rights, they encourage them to focus on creating and adhering to "best practices," or core standards, which will improve the working standard as a whole.

OUTSOURCING

Large scale business also opens up the possibility of outsourcing. Outsourcing is when a company moves part of their business to another location (generally the term is used to describe outsourcing to outside the country which they are located in). For example, it is much cheaper for a company to manufacture their toys in China than it is in the United States. They may choose to outsource their manufacturing to China and have the toys shipped back to the United States for distribution. Another example is that many companies find it cheaper to have their customer support lines in countries other than the United States where a higher minimum wage is enforced. As an example of in-country outsourcing, some companies will hire a security company to guard their buildings instead of creating their own security teams.

In many ways, outsourcing allows for increased efficiency in markets. From an economic standpoint, outsourcing can allow specialization. The idea behind specialization is that if each person does the thing that they are the best at then the economy as a whole will be able to produce more. The ability to outsource projects that would be expensive or difficult for the company to complete themselves allows the company to be more profitable. Considered in these terms, outsourcing is a responsibility of a company if it wants to maximize the returns to stockholders.

Outsourcing can also be a great benefit to those who are receiving the jobs. For example, if a company is to build a factory in a rural area in an underdeveloped nation it would bring jobs and stability to the area, as well as benefitting the company if it reduces their costs. Decreasing costs to the company can also bring benefits to consumers because the end price of the product or service will also likely decrease as a result. Therefore outsourcing can be a benefit to everyone involved.

In addition to increasing efficiency and decreasing prices, outsourcing allows companies to access resources that they would otherwise not have had, and allows them to focus on the core parts of their business. Outsourcing is not just something that is done by American companies. True, companies in the United States find it profitable to outsource production to other areas of the world with cheap labor, but other areas of the world are equally benefitted by use of American companies.

For example, large machinery items and jets and airplanes are almost exclusively produced in the United States. Also, many people either hire American programmers and engineers or send them to schools in the United States to learn the skills that they need. In this way outsourcing allows access to resources that would not be found otherwise. Outsourcing allows companies to focus on the core parts of their business because they do not have to expend the resources it would take to perform the outsourced operations themselves and they can therefore work on developing or perfecting new products.

Although outsourcing can be very beneficial for companies, it is also often criticized and can become an ethical concern. For example, by outsourcing call centers to other countries, people worry that they will have to deal with unqualified representatives. If consumers try to use a help line provided by a company but because of language differences cannot understand the employee that they are speaking to, they will become frustrated and upset.

This means that although it saves the company money, it also reduces the efficiency and helpfulness and can create a bad reputation. Outsourcing is also criticized because many people feel that it moves much needed jobs to other countries simply for the sake of profits (however, from the standpoint of a stockholder the increased profits are a benefit so it depends on who is being asked whether it is a good or bad thing).

The ethical concerns involving outsourcing emerge as a result of the company's expansion. Language and cultural barriers become an issue, as well as the conflicts of differing legal standards between the countries in which the company operates. Security and fraud also become issues as the company will face increased exposure to problems as it expands. A company is often considered responsible for the actions of its employees and managing employees can be extremely difficult when a company spans countries or even continents.

One large ethical question facing multinational companies that outsource their operations is what labor standards that they should adhere to in their overseas businesses. The United States has some of the highest labor standards in the world – minimum wages, child labor laws, environmental considerations and working environment standards. Considered from an ethical standpoint it would be most logical for the business to conform to these higher standards in their businesses whether or not they are on United States soil. However, from a business standpoint the regulations can be very expensive for the business. As far as profit is concerned, the smarter decision is to adhere only to the standards expected by the country which the business is in. This causes quite an ethical problem.

One act that works to keep standards high for companies that are based in the United States but have operations overseas is the Alien Tort Claims Act. The Alien Tort Claims Act (ATCA) allows foreign citizens to bring a citizen of the United States to trial in the United States. For example, the act was used by a Paraguayan citizen to sue a police officer who had tortured a person in Paraguay. The acts uses have also begun extending to multinational corporations and preventing them from engaging in illegal business practices outside of the United States.

Part of the ethical problem that arises when companies outsource is that they do not always have direct control over the operations that are outsourced. For example, Nike outsourced production to factories overseas and it came to light that the company employed children in sweatshop like conditions.

The criticism of Nike was overwhelming and the company had to work to overcome the negative reputation and lawsuits that followed. One of the key questions was whether or not Nike should be held responsible for the conditions in the factory, when they technically were not owners and therefore (in their opinion) not responsible. However, the company has worked to improve conditions and its reputation.

In summary, the ethical concerns that face companies as they expand to multiple countries become increasingly complex and hard to solve. Because there is no single governing force and cultures across the world are so various it is nearly impossible to create a single set of ethical standards that all people will adhere to. However, despite difficulties, people and organizations continue to work towards creating a set of generally accepted standards and educating people about issues such as bribery and other forms of corruption, discrimination and human rights abuses.

INSOURCING

Insourcing is the exact opposite of outsourcing. Insourcing occurs when a company takes a process that was completed outside the company, or outsourced, and begins to complete the project in house. For example, a company may choose to outsource their web design work to a professional company. Over time, they may decide that they will get better, faster results to website updates by having an internal employee perform the task.

Ecology and Global Business

On local, global and national scales, environmental issues can often come into play and raise ethical issues for businesses. The study of how these environmental factors affect people and how people interact with their environment is known as ecology.

Although ecology is rooted in biological study, considering topics such as biomass, and the development of organisms and ecosystems, it often becomes entwined with business considerations because it is impossible for people to avoid interacting with the environment around them.

As people become more aware of the implications of environmental problems, there is an increased movement of public opinion in favor of businesses that can label themselves or their products as "green," and a movement away from businesses that appear to be highly polluting or unsafe. It is therefore increasingly important that businesses consider the different environmental issues which affect their operations as a means of ensuring that their business is successful. In addition to the effects of environmental issues in the business sense, however, environmental issues are often a matter of ethics more than a matter of business. Some examples of ways that businesses pollute the environment include water pollution, emissions and consumption of scarce natural resources. Each type of pollution has accompanying adverse effects which should be considered.

WATER POLLUTION

Water pollution refers to the dumping of waste into nearby lakes or streams. This waste can take the form of toxic chemicals, raw sewage or other factors. Even in places where information about pollution is wide spread, such as in the United States, water pollution can still be a problem. The EPA classifies just over a third of all waterways (including lakes, rivers and coastal waters) in the United States as polluted.

The creation of water pollution is classified in two different ways: point sources and non-point sources. Non-point sources are the more difficult to identify and control of the two. A non-point source of pollution originates from various sources. Often non-point sources of pollution occur as a result of rainfall. For example, as rainfall moves through farmland it picks up fertilizers and the runoff moves into water sources becoming a hazard and contaminating the water. While clearly the pollution is a problem it can be impractical to stop all farmers from using fertilizer because that would create a whole new set of problems. It is also difficult or impossible to identify what is truly causing the problem because it can come from so many different sources. Another example of non-point source pollution is sediments. In this case, the runoff picks up loose silt or other small particles which cloud the water and stop light from penetrating the surface of the water. Underwater plants suffer as a result. This example demonstrates how difficult it can be to regulate non-point sources of pollution because they need not necessarily be a direct result of human actions.

In contrast to non-point sources, point sources are single, specific and identifiable sources of water pollution. For example, a factory which is built near a river and simply funnels their pollution via a pipe into that river. Another example could be if a boat were to sustain a leak and spill a large amount of oil into the water. Sewage treatment facilities and storm drains are also classified as point sources. In each of the mentioned situations the pollution is originated from an identifiable and (essentially) stationary source.

Because point sources of pollution can be identified relatively easily and more specifically, they are much easier to monitor and control. The EPA regulates water pollution through the Federal Water Pollution Control Act, more commonly referred to as the Clean Water Act. The act makes it illegal for anyone to dump waste in navigable waters unless they first obtain a permit. The permits are distributed through the National Pollutant Discharge Elimination System (NPDES) which is regulated by the EPA. It is important that businesses consider how water pollution issues may affect their operations and account for any time, equipment or measure that must be taken to ensure that all regulations are met.

AIR POLLUTION

Emissions, or air pollution, are also an important environmental issue to be considered by businesses. In a general sense, air pollution can be a particularly difficult and worrisome sort of pollution because it has such wide ranging effects. If the air in an area becomes polluted it affects everyone indiscriminately and it is extremely difficult to avoid. Everyone needs air and can only breathe in the air that is immediately around them. The EPA regulates air pollution through the Clean Air Act.

The Clean Air Act identifies and seeks to reduce three general types of emissions. One type of air pollution that the act focuses on is stopping the production of chemicals which are dangerous to the ozone layer in the earth's atmosphere. The ozone layer serves the important function of shielding the earth from ultraviolet (UV) rays from the sun. Not only do these rays cause sunburns, but they are linked to cataracts and skin cancer in humans in addition to having many adverse effects on the environment.

Compounds called chlorofluorocarbons (CFCs) can deplete the ozone layer, causing it to have gaps. As a result of this there are many regulations which monitor CFCs. For example, they used to be in aerosol cans and refrigerators, but due to government bans they have been removed from those products. As with all forms of pollution, however, completely eliminating CFCs would be expensive and difficult. In some cases there are no known substitutes for the use of CFCs, so their continued use is allowed.

Businesses which produce dangerous compounds, such as CFCs, which are released into the air should be sure that they take notice of the amounts which they produce. Looking beyond just the legal restrictions which may apply, it can also be considered an ethical issue in the fact that it has the potential to harm people. Ignoring possible pollution problems to save money can have irreversible consequences in the future. Just because something may be legal, doesn't make it ethically sound.

Another type of air pollution which the EPA seeks to reduce is the emission of compounds which are toxic to humans or which are carcinogenic (cancer-causing) in nature. This type of pollution is particularly relevant to business practices because the majority of this type of pollution originates through manmade sources like to factories or cars. Exposure to concentrated sources of these chemicals, or exposure over time, can have ill effects ranging from nausea and mild illness to death in extreme cases. The third type of pollution which the EPA is concerned with is just the reduction of general air pollution which causes smog, acid rain and other problems.

The EPA regulates the production of pollutants by commercial sources by issuing permits. Through this they can track and monitor potentially problematic sources of pollution. In addition, companies may be forced to pay fees based upon levels, amounts or types of pollution or meet certain restrictions in order to obtain a permit.

PRIMARY & SECONDARY POLLUTANTS

In terms of working to stop or reduce pollution, pollutants can be further classified into two different categories: primary pollutants and secondary pollutants. Primary pollutants are the simplest to regulate. They are basically the air pollution equivalent of point-source water pollution. That is, primary pollutants emanate from a specific source. More importantly, primary pollutants retain their chemical makeup. Primary pollutants don't react with other chemicals to create a problem, they just are a problem. Examples of primary pollutants include ash from burning things (or from volcanic eruptions), carbon monoxide from cars, ammonia, toxic metals or radioactive waste.

Secondary pollutants are harder to identify because they are pollutants which undergo a chemical change in the atmosphere. For example, smog is a result of secondary pollutants. Machines and factories don't pump "smog" into air – it evolves as a result of chemicals that get pumped into the air. Similarly, the production of ground level ozone is of concern. (Although in the atmosphere ozone protects against UV rays, at ground level it becomes a pollutant.)

ENVIRONMENTAL REGULATIONS

The Clean Water Act and Clean Air Act are just two examples of many regulations which work to reduce the effects of pollution. For example, some additional laws which relate to air and water pollution may establish regulations regarding the quality of drinking water, regulate the testing of potentially toxic products or restrict the use of harmful chemicals in pesticides and fertilizers used to produce food. They may also enact regulations to reduce the incidences of oil spills or require that adequate information be given to people in the area surrounding places where dangerous pollution is emitted. Regulations such as these are referred to as command and control regulations. Command and control regulations are regulations which dictate how a company should manage certain processes that pollute the environment. They are basically detailed regulations which are meant to reduce or eliminate pollution levels so that the fall into accord with federal expectations and mandates regarding the problem. The first step for any business to move toward more ethical environmental practices is to be aware of and in compliance with all environmental regulations.

Although it is not an actual law, the ISO 14001 is a standard that companies can voluntarily follow in improving their environmental safety. ISO stands for International Standardization Organization. The organization has standardizations for all different areas, but the 14001 standard applies to environmental issues. ISO 14001 is a voluntary program of continual improvement. It is not a specific standard which companies must meet, but rather provides a framework which businesses can use to get started. Under ISO 14001 a company develops its own set of objectives and goals. The company then implements processes in an effort to meet these goals. The company should then consider how well the processes are helping them meet their goals and find ways to continue to improve.

Another issue, in addition to the various regulations, which relevant to environmental practices is the idea of environmental racism. Environmental racism describes a situation in which environmental hazards affect different races differently. For example, a clustering of people of a certain minority group living in the part of town with the poorest air quality and worst housing would be an example of environmental racism. Environmental justice is a move toward equality among all races in issues relating to environmental risks and health.

Another problem that is faced by businesses that create a lot of pollution is that if they try and move into a residential area people may protest and try to prevent them from doing so. When people object to having something built near them it referred to as NIMBY, or "not in my backyard." For example, a chemical plant that is going in near an elementary school would most likely face objections by the people whose children attend the school.

One reason that it is easy for businesses to overlook or ignore the ill effects of pollution is because the cost of pollution is external to their operations. In other words, the business produces the pollution, but the ill effects which manifest as a result are paid by the community. This is one reason why pollution could be considered unethical – the business is imposing costs on others through their operations. It is also difficult to determine what the exact costs are of the pollution. Often times the ill effects occur in the future, so there is no way to really judge how they will unfold or what the severity will be. In another sense it is also difficult to really quantify the costs of pollution because every person has a different opinion about what a reasonable effort at reducing pollution is.

Both air and water pollution are problems which can be created as a result of things that a business produces, however the use of natural resources can also become a problem. In considering pollution the worry is about what is being put into the environment, and potentially harming individuals and destroying fragile environments. However, also of large concern in many manufacturing businesses is the use of naturally produced raw materials such as wood or oil. The overuse of these natural materials causes just as many problems as the overproduction of dangerous substances.

SUSTAINABLE DEVELOPMENT

The term sustainable development is used to describe practices which use resources at a rate which meets current needs and prepares for future needs. In other words, sustainable development is not exploiting resources to an extent that they will be unavailable to future generations. For example, a large tree that grows over the course of a century can be cut down and used to fuel a fire relatively easily and quickly. However, if a fire is needed once again the next day, that tree will obviously not have replenished itself (i.e., it will not have regrown). Compound this incident over years of logging to produce everything from homes to paper to firewood and the result is large scale deforestation of some areas. In this example the resource, trees, are being used at a rate that is faster than they are naturally produced at. A state such as this is referred to as environmental degradation.

In some cases the overuse of a resource is more harmful than in others. For example, with resources such as plants or animal populations, the growth of the resource is geometric. In other words, the more there are the faster they grow (like with the human population). It therefore follows that the effect would be reversed as the resource is used. The more cows or chickens that are consumed by people, the fewer there are to regrow populations and the slower the rate they can be replenished at. Because of this it is important that businesses have an accurate understanding of the resources that they use, and the different issues that come into play with them.

Resources that are easily replenished can be referred to as renewable resources. For example, solar energy is a renewable form of energy. Because the sun will always continue to shine during the daytime, and using it to create energy one day will not affect the ability to do so the next day. Many resources, however, are non-renewable. The classic example of a non-renewable resource is fossil fuels. Fossil fuels are so named because they develop from dead organic materials. Although they do form naturally, they do so through a process which takes millions of years to complete. Because of this for all practical purposes fossils fuels are a resource which cannot be renewed. This can be worrisome because many of the energy forms that are encountered on a daily basis such as gasoline or coal are forms of fossil fuels.

For other resources it can be more difficult to classify them as either renewable or non-renewable. An example of this is arable land. Arable land is land which can be used for agricultural purposes. In one sense the land is a renewable resource – it can be used year after year. However, it could also be argued that it is a non-renewable resource. Minerals and things in the soil that help crops to grow can be depleted if the land is overused. Things such as fertilizers or certain farming techniques can combat this process, but if it isn't addressed the land can become useless. Again, it can take thousands of years for the land to naturally renew itself, so in this situation it could be considered a non-renewable resource.

Other resources do not necessarily take as long to produce, or they are not used up as quickly. For example, although a tree takes years to grow, it may produce apples each year. Therefore, it makes sense to eat those apples each year based on the amount that grow. If apples are considered to be a natural resource, then this would be an example of an equilibrium environment. Apples are consumed each year at a rate which is equal to the rate at which they can be produced. However, in this example the equilibrium state is essentially forced – the apples cannot be saved for future years, nor can more apples than are currently produced be consumed. In the case of natural resources such as oil, endangered species or trees there is nothing stopping people from overusing the resource.

Another example of an equilibrium environment is a Christmas tree business. Christmas trees take years to grow, so it requires that the business owner carefully consider future consumption needs and current needs in deciding which trees to cut down and which to let grow for another year. They must ensure that the trees are replenished by planting new trees each year to make up for those which were cut down.

The owner would wish to produce just enough trees each year to meet the demands of customers – equilibrium. However, there is nothing actually stopping them from cutting down all of the trees in a single season if there is a very high demand for the trees and they decide that it would be the most profitable option for them. Because of this, the equilibrium consumption is somewhat harder to effectively determine and sustain. People don't always use the same amount of a resource from year to year.

If a resource were to be used at rate slower than it could be replenished this would describe a state of economic renewal. In this state the resource would be able to increase in abundance, meaning there would be plenty for any future consumption needs as well. For example, if for some reason everyone in the world decided that they would no longer use oil, than the rate of consumption would be zero. Therefore, the oil supplies within the earth would be able to increase over time. Clearly this would be the most environmentally preferable option, however in some cases it is not economically feasible, or economically preferable, due to the various uses of the resource.

Each of the three states – environmental degradation, environmental equilibrium and environmental renewal – correspond with a different level of economic sustainability. If a resource is in a state of environmental degradation it will eventually be depleted. Therefore, the use of the resource is not economically sustainable. Eventually the economy will reach a critical point because it will be dependent on a resource that is no longer available. Here is one area where business ethics comes into play. Although there are not always laws regulating the use of resources (since they may be private property), it would clearly be unethical to use a resource to its extinction. Not only would the costs of overuse be paid by individuals in the future, but it could also cause unforeseen problems with the environment.

Environmental equilibrium is clearly a preferred state to environmental degradation, but it does come with its problems as well. A resource which is used in a state of environmental equilibrium creates what is called a stable state economy. This is because the use of the resource is stable. The economy could continue to use the resource at that rate and not have to worry about possible depletion problems. However, even though it is technically a sustainable state, this is a precarious situation. Determining the equilibrium rate can be quite difficult for a number of reasons. Firstly, the amount that people demand can change over time. An amount of resources that sustains the population now will be insufficient when the population grows. Also, if new mineral deposits or mines or animal populations are discovered then the rate at which it is replenished may change based on the new information. Because of these and other factors it isn't always feasible to just require that environmental equilibrium be attained.

A state of environmental renewal is generally the most preferred and sustainable situation of the three. Because the resource is used at a rate that allows it to grow, it allows for current use in combination with the fact that it prepares for future growth and development. A state of environmental renewal eliminates the problems that plague equilibrium and degradation markets because not only is the resource not in danger of being eliminated, but changes in populations or demands are not as much of a worry.

It is important to recognize, however, that achieving a state effective for sustainable development does not have to mean that people must sacrifice and use less of a resource or that its use is restricted by law. Rather, it means that people need to find innovating and effective ways of using the resource more efficiently. For example, hybrid cars that run on both gas and electricity reduce people's dependence on gas (a scarce natural resource) and could be considered a step towards sustainable development. Through technological innovations such as this people, and businesses, may continue to use the resources without being completely dependent on them or without having to use them at as high of a rate.

An important element of sustainable development is that it encourages the development of newer and more efficient technologies, rather than quick fixes or small improvements on existing technologies that are known to be unsustainable. This is true not only of sustainable consumption of resources, but also of pollution. High levels of pollution can be considered to be an unsustainable practice in the sense that they "consume" clean air, water and environments. This move from polluting and inefficient practices to energy conscious and clean practices can be expensive, consume time and resources and can be a hassle. So, the question becomes about whether there are any benefits or encouraging factors associated with a business in doing so.

One benefit of more energy efficient business practices and technologies is that in the long run they tend to reduce energy costs, even if they seem expensive in the short run. Another cost saving aspect is with the disposal of waste. Companies that produce large amounts of garbage or waste have to dispose of it in some way. At least in the United States, the disposal of waste is regulated and can become expensive. In effect, the problem of disposing of waste means that companies which produce waste end up double paying – once for the initial materials and again to get rid of the excess. Reducing waste eliminates the hassle and cost of disposing of waste. Minimizing the production of waste by using raw materials more carefully contributes to this benefit and reduces the strain on the environment. In addition, in some cases there are tax breaks for companies that institute more environmental practices.

Sound environmental practices can also be essential in developing good relations with customers and employees. As consumers become increasingly informed and aware of environmental issues it becomes increasingly advantageous for companies to display environmental awareness. This extends to people in the community, shareholders, suppliers and all stakeholders in general. In addition, just as employees tend to be more loyal and efficient when they believe their employers to practice good business ethics, they are likely increase performance when they believe their employers to have ethical environmental practices.

Another consideration is that when businesses do ensure that they are using sustainable practices they are really benefitting themselves. By ensuring that resources will be available in the future the business is effectively ensuring that they will be able to continue their operations in the future. If a business does not consider and protect its own long run interests by considering environmental effects, they will eventually have to face the consequences of that.

In short, in the long run sustainable practices prove to be beneficial to companies because it ensures that they will be able to operate in the future. Businesses should take environmental concerns into consideration when coordinating their operations because of concerns on various levels. On a legal level of responsibility, businesses should be aware of and in compliance with any regulations that are pertinent to their operations.

On an ethical level businesses should consider the possible ill effects which their operations produce that are external to their operations. Finally, on a business level it is important and beneficial for companies to consider whether or not their operations are such that they can be sustained over time.

 Business and Government

There are many ways in which government and politics overlap. Political movements can have a great effect on businesses because of the many different laws and regulations which dictate how a company can operate. There are laws regarding the environment which mandate the levels and amounts and types of waste which companies can dispose of and how they are to dispose of it. There are laws which govern companies in their interactions with employees – such as laws setting minimum wage standards, age limitations and safety guidelines. There are even laws which regulate the ways in which companies can expand, such as procompetitive laws among others. Additionally, publicly traded corporations must produce financial statements regulated by the SEC and pay corporate taxes.

Clearly business and politics cannot be effectively separated from one another. The question becomes whether the intrusions of government into businesses and the economy in general is detrimental or if it is actually preferable. While the answer to this question is really a matter of opinion, there are a number of factors to consider. For example, one instance in which the intervention of governments into business is often considered preferable is when the business is imposing external costs on the community. If there are external costs, such as was mentioned with pollution, then the company will be creating costs which they do not have to pay. Therefore, it becomes a burden to society. Here governments can intervene by forcing companies to consider these costs so that the burden to society is lessened. For example, if the company has to pay a certain tax or fee based on the amount that they pollute, then effectively the cost of pollution is returned back to the company. This will result in a more efficient operation of the market as a whole.

Another example of a case in which government intervention is often considered preferable is when a single company gains too much power, such as in a monopoly. In economics terms this is described as a company gaining market power. If a company has market power than they are able to increase their prices above what the price would be in a competitive situation. Therefore, by ensuring that companies do not use unethical methods to put competitors out of business, and by prosecuting companies which collude with one another in order to keep prices artificially high, the government can aid in ensuring that prices are kept at a more reasonable level.

The difficulty with regulations on monopolies is determining whether or not a company truly has market power. If a company drives all of their competitors out of business through unethical practices than clearly a monopoly has formed. However, in some cases a company need not be the only company to have market power – just a large portion.

One example of this is the merger between Northwest Airlines and Delta Air Lines in 2008. When the two companies merged they were under a lot of scrutiny because it meant that the resulting company – which kept the Delta name – would be the largest airline in the world. After deliberating it was decided that because the two companies were primarily focused in different areas, and their merge would most likely bring airline prices down, that the merger did not create a monopoly.

GOVERNMENT IMPOSED QUALITY STANDARDS

Government control over potentially harmful products is also very useful to consumers. There were times in United States history when the government didn't place any quality or health standards on the handling of meat products, or the standards of drinking water. For example, prior to 1891 there were absolutely no government regulations regarding the handling of meat. This resulted in inadequate measures to ensure the safety of meat products. Because the measures were inadequate it was not uncommon that people could get sick from eating contaminated meat. Because there was no law demanding certain standards be kept, there was no legal basis from which a person could seek recourse. If they did get sick, they were just unlucky but couldn't act. However, after the institution of policies regarding meat there were many additional policies which were created to further ensure that many different types of products were handled safely.

This practice continues today with the government setting standards on pharmaceutical testing to ensure safe medications are developed, water quality standards, food quality standards, labels for dangerous toys and machinery and many other things as well. Also, safety standards and age limitations for dangerous workplaces are government regulated. The fact that the government monitors these things protects consumers and results in improved technologies and safer products and practices.

GOVERNMENT INTERVENTION

Import tariffs are another case in which governments can intervene in a market. However, in this case the effects can vary. For example, if the price of good such as wheat can be obtained at a lower price from other countries, people will obviously choose to buy the lower priced wheat. However, this means that wheat farmers in the United States will suffer. In this case consumers would prefer that the government not intervene – they benefit from the cheaper prices of imported wheat. On the other hand, producers of wheat in the United States would clearly prefer that the government chose to impose a tariff, or tax, on wheat which is shipped to the United States from other countries. This would make their wheat more comparable in price which means that they wouldn't lose business.

Alternatively, if the price of wheat is lower in the United States than in other areas of the world, then the situation reverses itself. In this case it would be the producers of wheat that would want the government to do nothing. They benefit from being able to sell their wheat to other countries at a higher profit margin. On the other hand, consumers would want a tax to be placed on companies that shipped their goods outside of the country to make it less profitable. This way the companies would be less likely to do so and the price could go down. Once again there is disagreement which arises as to whether or not the government should intervene in economic and business related affairs.

One example of a government intervention of the economy is President Bill Clinton's failed attempt at health care reform in 1993. Clinton proposed a health care bill which would require health insurance. It would carefully control the maximum rates and force insurance companies to compete for customers. However, for numerous reasons, the bill failed. Part of the problem with the bill was its timing. In the early 1990's the economy was pulling out of a recession. People were worried about prices and the market in general. Clinton was elected and quickly got working on the bill, however by the time it was finally finished ten months later people weren't as worried anymore and were less interested in health care reform.

They worried that the bill would be a burden to small businesses which could afford to pay for employee health coverage. Therefore, there were economic reasons why the bill failed. There were also political reasons. Many members of Congress were upset that the bill was basically entirely written by an executive committee instead of by members of Congress, so they had little say in it. Another reason for the failure of the bill was that it was also strongly opposed by health insurance companies, which ran ads against the policy and worked to generate a negative opinion of it. Here the interactions between business and politics are more complex than just a single issue. Both work with and against each other in different situations.

Although people typically think of business interactions with politicians as a form of corruption, that doesn't have to be the case. Corporations do have the right to support candidates and causes that they agree with or that will benefit them. It would be ridiculous to expect that companies not promote candidates that they believe will bring greater economic prosperity and make things better for the business. The problem is that it can be difficult to differentiate between when a company is unethically bribing a politician and one which honestly supports the politician and believes that they are the best option. But it is important to remember that there are ways in which corporations can influence politicians and have a positive overall impact.

When it comes to economic problems often businesses can have a better understanding of what the barriers are to economic growth and progress than politicians do. It is therefore beneficial for the two groups to work together to achieve common goals for mutual benefits. For example, during difficult economic times often companies can work with government officials to get regulations passed which help businesses to expand or operate more easily, bringing economic growth. Or, as in the case of President Clinton's health care bill, companies can oppose regulatory actions that they consider detrimental.

It can also be difficult to determine the role of government in regulating ethical issues. It would be counterproductive to repeal laws that regulate ethical issues such as truth in advertising, truth in lending or insider trading. Although these laws do essentially force ethical behavior it is a benefit to society as a whole and can even be helpful to companies. However, if the government were to regulate every ethical issue that faced a business it would be going a little too far. Businesses would not be able to be creative or innovative if every move they made were controlled by the government.

One such issue for which the balance between regulation and company choice can be difficult to find is matters of pollution. While a certain amount of regulation is necessary to ensure public safety, such as laws regulating food and water quality or laws dictating procedures related to the disposal of radioactive waste, there is also a point where it is crippling to business to regulate pollution laws further. There are many people that believe that laws regulating pollution should be reduced to allow companies to produce at lower costs and thereby lower prices to the market. However, there are also many people who believe that no amount of pollution is acceptable and believe that the regulations should only be tightened. Because there are so many opinions there is no single answer to whether or not government regulations are beneficial and desirable or detrimental.

One theory that stands in opposition to the idea that government interventions can be beneficial is class theory. **Classical theory** follows the belief that the economy is self-correcting. It relies on the laws of supply and demand to regulate the economy. This view, therefore, implies that any actions by the government will only make matters worse and less efficient. The term for an economy in which transaction are not regulated by the government is a laissez faire economy. Laissez faire is a French term which literally means to "let do." In other words, it refers to the fact that the government allows the economy to fluctuate naturally. While this approach would leave the market open to possible problems such as monopolies or unethical business practices, it also has many compelling arguments in its favor. To a large extent a capitalist economy such as the United States relies on a laissez faire approach.

Capitalism requires that individuals own property, and use it to improve their own well-being. If companies are unable to seek their own best interests and profits, the capitalist system falls apart. Also, if government regulations stop or impede change then the system is harmed as well. In a laissez faire capitalist system, if a company is doing poorly then they will go out of business. This allows new and more effective companies to take their place and the market as a whole benefits and continues to improve over time. If governments intervene by "bailing out" companies, then this natural cycle is circumvented to the detriment of the market as a whole. A suffering company does not operate efficiently.

Although in the case of problems such as monopolies or importation and exportation government regulations can be useful, there are clearly many ways in addition to just bail outs of failing companies in which government regulations are actually harmful to effective markets. An additional example could be taxes. This is because when the government places a tax on an item it essentially drives a wedge between the suppliers and the consumers. This is because the suppliers, or businesses, are providing the goods and services at a certain price, but the price that customers have to pay is higher than the price companies receive. Because of this wedge the market won't operate efficiently, with either the companies or the customers (or some mix of the two) having to bear the weight of the tax.

That businesses (and individuals) have to pay income taxes also distorts the flow of money in a market. Because people have less money they will consume fewer products, meaning that businesses will be able to make less money on top of the fact that they have to pay taxes on what they do make. As a direct result companies have less money to invest in expansion and increasing production and efficiency. (This isn't to say that taxes are inherently entirely bad. The government provides many useful functions and must raise some revenue in order to do so.)

That there are so many pros and cons to government intrusions into business and economic matters the balance is a tenuous one. In some cases government actions can improve conditions between businesses and consumers, but it is also true that in many cases actions by the government just make interactions more difficult and inefficient. With some cases the actions are simultaneously harmful and beneficial. Even in cases in which the government's actions are beneficial – such as pollution reduction – there are still arguments that it is not strictly the job of the government to act and that it should be worked out in other ways.

Any time that the government considers a new policy which will affect the economy it is important that they carefully weigh the balance between costs and benefits of the policy. For example, a regulation which requires companies to reduce pollution a certain amount which will cost three billion dollars to fulfill, should have predicted benefits which exceed three billion dollars for the policy to be considered reasonable and beneficial. If the costs of the policy exceed the expected benefits of the policy then it should be dismissed.

BUSINESS AND POLITICS

Thus far only the ways in which governments interfere with business operations have been discussed, but there are also many ways in which businesses can influence political matters. Most often the influence of businesses over government officials is considered in terms of how it can be a source of corruption. For example, businesses flat out bribing politicians or influencing their decisions through campaign contributions or lobbying. Each of these situations has a number of regulations and loopholes associated with it through which companies can find ways to affect political outcomes.

Bribery through campaign contributions is one of the first things to come to mind when considering the ways that businesses interfere with political actions. In the early days of the United States, candidates in elections didn't campaign the way they do now. However, as the country grew elections as they are today began to evolve. Most importantly the amount of capital and resources necessary for a candidate to run for office became increasingly large. Today's presidential campaigns spend anywhere in the range of hundreds of millions of dollars to billions of dollars. Because corporations have access to larger amounts of capital than does the average person, their contributions to political campaigns can make a significant difference.

Understanding how companies contribute money to campaigns requires an understanding of the terms hard money and soft money as it relates to campaign donations.

Hard money is money legally donated to a candidate to be specifically used for the purpose of campaigning. Corporations have every right to donate money to political candidates that they support, just as an individual has the right to do so. However, the amounts of hard money which both corporations and individuals are allowed to donate are limited by law.

Soft money is distinguished from hard money in that it is money which is donated to political parties and used for party building purposes. Essentially the difference between the two is that hard money is donated to candidates and hard money is donated to political parties. Soft money contributions are not limited by law.

The first act which made a significant effort to restrict campaign contributions was the Federal Election Campaign Act. The act was first passed in 1971 and later amended in 1974. The act was meant to reduce campaign spending and limit campaign contributions. (Initially it banned all corporate donations altogether, but that was changed to specific limitations when it was amended.) The act also dictated that campaign contributions amounting to more than ten thousand dollars must be reported by the campaign and created the Federal Election Commission (FEC) to enforce the law.

Because of the limits on hard money contributions, soft money became a loophole method for corporations to aid the campaigns of candidates they supported legally. Instead of directly donating the money to the candidate they would donate the money to the party. As long as the money wasn't used specifically as part of the candidate's campaign its use was unregulated. In other words, if the party aired a TV commercial which promoted the issues supported by the candidate but didn't specifically tell voters which candidate to vote for it was classified as soft money. It could also be classified as soft money if all it did was criticize the opposing candidate, it just couldn't support a specific candidate.

Another loophole that developed was special interest groups (SIGs) and political action committees (PACs). A special interest group is any group which uses involvement in politics to further their beliefs and positions. Special interest groups do this by organizing political action committees. PACs are groups that supported a specific issue or candidate, but were not technically part of their campaign. Therefore, a company (or group of people or union) could set up its own PAC and donate unlimited sums of money to it. The PAC could then use that money to campaign for a particular candidate or support an issue or really anything that it wanted to. As long as the PACs efforts weren't coordinated with or tied to a specific politician than it was not limited in its ability to campaign.

Additional loopholes came in the form of independent expenditures and issue ads. A company would use its own funds (independent expenditures) in order to run ads (called issue ads) or other things promoting a certain candidate. The ads could promote issues or criticize candidates or viewpoints. They could even specifically discuss a certain candidate and their viewpoints. As long as the company didn't specifically promote a candidate or encourage voters to support them then the efforts were not limited by hard money contribution laws. It's basically the situation as with a PAC, but the company spends its money directly as opposed to donating it to a PAC.

Another way that corporations can help with campaigns is through in kind contributions. In a general sense, in kind contributions are when a person or company trades goods or services in place of money. For example, often people are more comfortable donating humanitarian supplies (blankets, canned food, etc) than they are donating money to a humanitarian service. It would be considered an in kind contribution because it helps and supports the organization, but allows the person to know how their contributions are being used. In kind contributions can be a way of aiding political campaigns without any money changing hands if, for example, a broadcasting company airs political messages for free. This is clearly an aid to the campaign, but no money changes hands.

As the number of loopholes through which contributions could come came to light, the federal government began taking additional actions to limit them. The Bipartisan

Campaign Reform Act (BCRA) was designed to further restrict the amount that could be spent on a political campaign. The act was designed to effectively ban the use of soft money in campaigns. It also specifically prohibited issue ads (or "non-partisan" ads) from being run during times around elections.

In addition to campaign contributions, companies also influence political actions through lobbying. Lobbying involves meeting with senators, representatives, staff members or other important people in order to state your point of view and persuade them to vote how you wish them to. The term doesn't only apply to corporations but it is a common way that they can influence politicians.

Sample Test Questions

1) Which of the following companies was NOT implicated in a scandal in the early 2000s?

    A) Enron
    B) Coca-Cola
    C) Tyco International
    D) All of the above were implicated in scandals

The correct answer is D:) All of the above were implicated in scandals. Due to the various different scandals occurring in the early 2000s, federal regulations concerning businesses were tightened. One example of this is the Sarbanes-Oxley Act.

2) Command and control regulations

    A) Prevent a person in a position of power from exploiting their power for their own benefit.
    B) Allow a lawyer to withdraw legal representation for their client.
    C) Regulate how a company should manage certain processes that pollute the environment.
    D) Make it illegal for any person to bribe a foreign official.

The correct answer is C:) Regulate how a company should manage certain processes that pollute the environment.

3) The purpose of the International Monetary Fund is to

    A) Help developing countries strengthen their economies.
    B) Prevent international trade crises.
    C) Loan money to individual banks so that they don't go bankrupt.
    D) Meticulously track the flow of currency from country to country.

The correct answer is B:) Prevent international trade crises. It regulates the trade deficits of countries, and can loan them money if it is necessary.

4) Considered from an ethical standpoint, MNCs should

   A) Conform to the labor standards of the country in which the particular business operates.
   B) Conform to the highest standards in all businesses whether overseas or not.
   C) Pick and choose with its businesses which laws to conform to.
   D) Refuse to engage in outsourcing as it can only be harmful to the origin country's economy.

The correct answer is B:) Conform to the highest standards in all businesses whether overseas or not. However, this can be expensive and hinder the business' effectiveness. Therefore, the ethical and financial interests are at odds.

5) Which of the following describes a type of conflict of interest where a broker owns securities and spreads rumors about them to make the price go up, then sells them before the price goes back down?

   A) Pump and dump
   B) Family interest
   C) Self-dealing
   D) Outside employment

The correct answer is A:) Pump and dump.

6) Which of the following is TRUE about spam?

   A) It is messages sent electronically to a large number of people.
   B) It is unsolicited.
   C) It can be send through email, instant messaging, blogs or other electronic methods.
   D) All of the above

The correct answer is D:) All of the above.

7) Business ethics is

   A) A highly specialized brand of ethics which focuses on the correctness of businesses contributing to political campaigns.
   B) A branch within most companies which works to ensure that employees are not cheating the business in any way.
   C) An attempt to apply moral and ethical principles to business actions.
   D) None of the above

The correct answer is C:) An attempt to apply moral and ethical principles to business actions. Although answer A may be one area to which business ethics could be applied, answer C is the most correct.

8) A noisy withdrawal would be done by which of the following?

   A) Lawyers
   B) Police officers
   C) Managers
   D) All of the above

The correct answer is A:) Lawyers. A noisy withdrawal is when a lawyer becomes aware of frauds committed by their client and withdraws legal representation for their client.

9) Noisy withdrawal is

   A) The study of designing more comfortably or easily used equipment.
   B) When a person is in a position to exploit their power for their own benefit.
   C) A moral theory which claims that the morality of an action is determined by the morality of the action itself – regardless of the consequence.
   D) When a lawyer withdraws legal representation for their client and notifies the proper authorities.

The correct answer is D:) When a lawyer withdraws legal representation for their client and notifies the proper authorities.

10) What is environmental justice?

   A) When companies consider environmental issues when they make business decisions.
   B) When issues are brought before a court which involve environmental factors.
   C) A move toward equality among all races in issues relating to environmental hazards.
   D) A collective movement by governments worldwide to decrease the emission of greenhouse gases.

The correct answer is C:) A move toward equality among all races in issues relating to environmental hazards.

11) A conflict of interest is

   A) The study of designing more comfortably or easily used equipment.
   B) When a person is in a position to exploit their power for their own benefit.
   C) A moral theory which claims that the morality of an action is determined by the morality of the action itself – regardless of the consequence.
   D) When a lawyer withdraws legal representation for their client and notifies the proper authorities.

The correct answer is B:) When a person is in a position to exploit their power for their own benefit.

12) A software designer knows that there are some minor problems with the software they are developing. However, if they wait to declare the product finished, it will not be released before another similar product, which would be highly damaging to its success. From the standpoint of an act utilitarian, the person would most likely

   A) Consider the people that will be using the software and wait to release it because it would not be fair to them to sell a damaged product.
   B) Decide that the benefits of releasing the software now outweigh the costs, and present the product as finished.
   C) Release the software even with its flaws because their good intentions of protecting the products popularity absolve them of any feeling of dishonesty.
   D) None of the above

The correct answer is B:) Decide that the benefits of releasing the software now outweigh the costs, and present the product as finished.

13) The CEO of a company works to raise stock prices because they will get a bonus if stock prices increase by a certain percentage. Which of Kohlberg's stages are they in?

   A) Stage 2
   B) Stage 3
   C) Stage 4
   D) Stage 6

The correct answer is A:) Stage 2. In this stage, people are most concerned with obtaining rewards, such as a bonus because of a rise in stock prices.

14) If a person owns a cupcake business and works in a cupcake factory, what type of conflict of interest is it considered?

   A) Pump and dump
   B) Family interest
   C) Self-dealing
   D) Outside employment

The correct answer is D:) Outside employment. This is when a person has two jobs which conflict with each other.

15) Which of the following terms describes a moral theory which derives morality from actions?

   A) Teleological ethics
   B) Consequentialism
   C) Deontological ethics
   D) None of the above

The correct answer is C:) Deontological ethics. Deontological ethics claims that the morality of an action is determined by the morality of the action itself – regardless of the consequence.

16) Which of the following statements is TRUE?

   A) According to teleological ethics an action's morality is determined based on its consequence.
   B) According to Kantian ethics an action's morality is determined based on its consequence.
   C) According to deontological ethics an action's morality is independent of its consequence.
   D) According to consequentialism an action's morality is independent of its consequence.

The correct answer is A:) According to teleological ethics an action's morality is determined based on its consequence. Teleology is a type of consequentialism.

17) Which of the following best describes soft money?

   A) Money that is donated to political parties for the purpose of party building activities.
   B) Money that the government injects into the economy for a short time to stimulate investment.
   C) Money that is donated to political candidates to help fund their campaigns.
   D) Money that is not based on the gold standard, but rather holds its value on the faith of citizens.

The correct answer is A:) Money that is donated to political parties for the purpose of party building activities. It used to be that soft money was not regulated as strictly and it was an easy way for wealthy individuals and corporations to get around hard money contribution limits.

18) Which of the following situations would be considered moral under Kantian theory?

   A) Studying for a test because you know that if you do, then you will do well on the test.
   B) Stealing from a store because you know that if you do then you will have nicer things and be happier.
   C) Helping an elderly neighbor because you feel sorry that they have no one to help them.
   D) Telling the truth because you think that it is the right thing to do.

The correct answer is D:) Telling the truth because you think that it is the right thing to do. Kant believed that emotions and consequences were irrelevant to morality.

19) The president of a company must decide whether to continue to sell textbooks that he knows have incorrect information in them or not. Considered from the standpoint of Kantian ethics, the president would most likely

   A) Discontinue the sale of the textbooks because of a perceived responsibility to society.
   B) Continue the sale of the textbooks because as a general rule the practice is not unconditional.
   C) Discontinue the sale of the textbooks because as a general rule the practice is not unconditional.
   D) Continue the sale of the textbooks because it would be detrimental to the company to cease sales.

The correct answer is C:) Discontinue the sale of the textbooks because as a general rule the practice is not unconditional.

20) A manager implements new safety procedures because they feel obligated to protect the safety of their employees. Which of Kohlberg's stages does this describe?

   A) Stage 3
   B) Stage 4
   C) Stage 5
   D) Stage 6

The correct answer is C:) Stage 5. In this stage, people act because they feel an obligation to society, like the manager feels an obligation to protect their workers.

21) Which of the following is a standard which aids companies in improving their environmental practices?

   A) ISO 14001
   B) ISO 2052
   C) Clean Air and Water Act
   D) Both A and B

The correct answer is A:) ISO 14001. ISO 14001 is a voluntary standard which attempts to aid companies in creating continually improving practices.

22) Hiring family members would be considered which type of conflict of interest?

A) Pump and dump
B) Nepotism
C) Outside employment
D) Self-dealing

The correct answer is B:) Nepotism. Nepotism, or family interest, refers to considering the interests of family ahead of what is truly best for the business. It can occur in terms of hiring, firing, promoting, employment benefits or other factors.

23) The Alien Tort Claims Act

A) Regulates the marketing and sale of potentially dangerous products.
B) Prevents U.S. citizens from exercising legal rights in foreign countries.
C) Creates equal trade of agricultural products among all nations.
D) Allows foreign citizens to bring a citizen of the United States to trial in the United States.

The correct answer is D:) Allows foreign citizens to bring a citizen of the United States to trial in the United States. This is useful for preventing multinational corporations for engaged in illegal business practices in countries outside the United States.

24) Which of the following is NOT a type of loophole that developed in response to limitations placed on hard money contributions?

A) Issue ads
B) Non-point source contributions
C) PACs
D) Independent expenditures

The correct answer is B:) Non-point source contributions. The correct term is non-point source pollution and it is not related to campaign contributions.

25) The purpose of the World Bank is to

   A) Help developing countries strengthen their economies.
   B) Prevent international trade crises.
   C) Loan money to individual banks so that they don't go bankrupt.
   D) Monitor the flow of valuable materials from country to country.

The correct answer is A:) Help developing countries strengthen their economies. The World Bank has the responsibility of fostering economic development. It loans with the purpose of the countries using that money to grow economically and then be able to pay back the loan.

26) A person helps an old lady across the street because they think that it is the right thing to do, and makes them feel useful and happy. Which of Kohlberg's stages are they in?

   A) Pre-conventional
   B) Conventional
   C) Nominal
   D) Post conventional

The correct answer is D:) Post conventional. In the post conventional stage, a person is ruled by conscience instead of society.

27) A child cleans their room so that they will be allowed to go to a friend's house. Which of Kohlberg's stages are they in?

   A) Pre-conventional
   B) Conventional
   C) Post conventional
   D) Nominal

The correct answer is A:) Pre-conventional. In the pre-conventional stage the main goal of a person is survival. The justification of actions comes from a simple understanding of punishment and reward systems.

28) Which of the following is NOT related to the interactions that occur between government and businesses?

   A) Bipartisan Campaign Reform Act
   B) Federal Election Campaign Act
   C) Truth in Advertising regulations
   D) All of the above are related to government and business interactions

The correct answer is D:) All of the above are related to government interactions. The laws named in answers A and B relate to how businesses can donate to political campaigns. Truth in advertising regulations are a way that governments regulate businesses.

29) Which of the following statements is NOT true?

   A) The debate over the ethics of bluffing is ongoing.
   B) It is only logical that a businessperson would feel obliged to in many cases to not share all of the information available to them, and to bluff where necessary to achieve the best outcome for the company.
   C) Any company that is caught bluffing in negotiations for government contracts is immediately brought under investigation by the SEC and those involved may face criminal charges.
   D) In many cases bluffing and deception can be a large hindrance to the progression of negotiations and just make it more difficult for all involved. It can also cause a bad reputation to be formed of an executive or company that would be detrimental.

The correct answer is C:) Any company that is caught bluffing in negotiations for government contracts is immediately brought under investigation by the SEC and those involved may face criminal charges.

30) Which of the following moral theories considers the action resulting in the greatest benefit to all people as the most moral action?

   A) Act utilitarianism
   B) Rule utilitarianism
   C) Relativism
   D) Deontology

The correct answer is A:) Act utilitarianism. This practice is called maximizing utility.

31) Cost benefit considerations would be most typical of which of type of ethics?

   A) Consequentialism
   B) Egoism
   C) Kantian
   D) Utilitarianism

The correct answer is D:) Utilitarianism. The idea behind utilitarianism is to "maximize utility." In other words the focus is on considering the benefits and costs and if the benefits are greater than the costs then the action is moral.

32) Which of the following acts conflict with the Privacy Act of 1974?

   A) Patriot Act
   B) U.S. Foreign Corrupt Practices Act
   C) Sarbanes-Oxley Act
   D) Bipartisan Campaign Reform Act

The correct answer is A:) Patriot Act.

33) Which of the following is NOT a responsibility that should be considered by businesses?

   A) Economic
   B) Fiduciary
   C) Philanthropic
   D) Legal

The correct answer is B:) Fiduciary. The four types of responsibility are economic, legal, ethical and philanthropic.

34) Which of the following statements is FALSE about the merger between Delta Air Lines and Northwest Airlines in 2008?

   A) The merge brought into question whether or not the new airline would have market power because it was the largest airline in the world.
   B) It was determined that the merge did not create a monopolistic situation because the two airlines were focused in different areas.
   C) Because Delta and Northwest are not the only two airlines there is no way that the merge could be considered anticompetitive.
   D) All of the above statements are true.

The correct answer is C:) Because Delta and Northwest are not the only two airlines there is no way that the merge could have been considered anticompetitive. If the merge had created a monopolistic situation, such as if Delta and Northwest were the only two airlines which had flights to New York (or another city), than the merge would have been anticompetitive.

35) Which of the following is NOT an example of how corporate espionage can occur?

   A) Hacking into a company's computer systems
   B) Bugging a competitor's office
   C) Digging through a competitor's trash cans
   D) All of the above are examples of corporate espionage

The correct answer is D:) All of the above are examples of corporate espionage.

36) Which type of responsibility is the LEAST regulated?

   A) Economic
   B) Legal
   C) Ethical
   D) Philanthropic

The correct answer is D:) Philanthropic. Because philanthropic responsibilities are essentially charitable acts, it is fundamentally impossible for there to be any sort of requirements or regulations surrounding them.

37) Corporate citizenship is

   A) A policy which demands that a company "gives back" to the communities in which it operates.
   B) The responsibility of a business to ensure the maximum returns to its investors.
   C) A system of accountability, oversight and control within the company.
   D) The consideration of large companies about the well-being of society when they make business decisions.

The correct answer is D:) The consideration of large companies about the well-being of society when they make business decisions. Corporate citizenship is also referred to as corporate social responsibility (CSR).

38) Which of the following statements about Corporate Social Responsibility is FALSE?

   A) It describes the consideration of large companies about the well being of society when they make business decisions.
   B) It is unanimously agreed that there is a dire need for it in today's society.
   C) It requires that companies consider people and the environment along with their own profit.
   D) All of the above statements are true.

The correct answer is B:) It is unanimously agreed that there is a dire need for it in today's society. Some feel that CSR disrupts the normal function of an economy and over regulates business practices. Others feel that this fact outweighs the negative impacts caused by irresponsible business practices.

39) Businesses with a mindset of "the customer is always right" often find themselves subject to more of which type of fraud?

   A) Consumer
   B) Accounting
   C) Marketing
   D) More than one of the above

The correct answer is A:) Consumer. A mindset of "the customer is always right" denotes that a company works to please and cater to its customers. This gives customers more room to manipulate or deceive the business.

40) Fossil fuels are a

   A) Renewable resource
   B) Non-point source pollutant
   C) Non-renewable resource
   D) Threat to environmental justice

The correct answer is C:) Non-renewable resource. Non-renewable resources are resources which either cannot be replenished, or which, like fossil fuels, take millions of years to do so.

41) The merger between Delta Air Lines and Northwest Airlines raised concerns about which of the following?

   A) Monopolies
   B) Government intervention in the economy
   C) Tariffs
   D) Subsidies

The correct answer is A:) Monopolies. The merger resulted in Delta becoming the largest airline in the world, and it had to be determined whether it would give them market power.

42) Ethical and philanthropic responsibilities are important in building

   A) Reputation
   B) Gross profit margins
   C) Corporate governance
   D) None of the above

The correct answer is A:) Reputation. Good ethics and philanthropic actions help a business in developing its reputation. A good reputation can take decades to develop, and can really make a difference in the success of a business. Reputation affects everyone from employees to investors to consumers. In a very real sense, a business's reputation can be what gives it its value.

43) If a resource is used at the same rate at which it can be replenished it is described as

   A) Environmental degradation
   B) Environmental neutralization
   C) Environmental equilibrium
   D) Environmental renewal

The correct answer is C:) Environmental equilibrium. Although this is obviously preferable to environmental degradation, it is a fairly precarious balance.

44) Which of the following is NOT a reason that President Clinton's attempt at health care reform in the early 1990s failed?

   A) Poor timing. The proposal took so long to complete that people weren't worried anymore.
   B) Ethics. Most people felt that the program (which charged more for middle class people) was highly unethical and would not support it.
   C) Politics. Congress members were annoyed that they had little involvement in its creation.
   D) All of the above are correct reasons for the failure.

The correct answer is B:) Ethics. Most people felt that the program (which charged more for middle class people) was highly unethical and would not support it. Timing and political reasons, along with the role of insurance corporations in criticizing it, played the largest role in the failure of the bill.

45) Which of the following is NOT an attempt at creating a universal ethical standard?

   A) Global Sullivan Principles
   B) United Nations Global Compact
   C) Caux Round Table
   D) Universal Ethics Protocol Organization

The correct answer is D:) Universal Ethics Protocol Organization. Principles of the Global Sullivan Principles include promoting equality and respect for human rights, refusing to accept bribes and ensuring employee safety. The GSP has been accepted by over 30 large companies. The UN's Global Compact similarly is signed by many large companies and focuses on protecting the environment, abolishing child labor and permitting unions to form. The Caux Round Table is an independent organization which works to teach and spread ethical practices to companies throughout the world.

46) Which of the following is NOT an example of social engineering?

A) Dumpster diving
B) Shoulder surfing
C) Password guessing
D) Phone eavesdropping

The correct answer is A:) Dumpster diving. Dumpster diving is a form of corporate espionage, but is not a form of social engineering. Shoulder surfing, password guessing and eavesdropping on phones are all common ways of social engineering however. Social engineering is using, tricking or deceiving individuals in an attempt to gain access to private information about a company.

47) Which of the following groups would not be considered a stakeholder?

A) Customers
B) Employees
C) Management
D) All of the above are stakeholders

The correct answer is D:) All of the above are stakeholders. Stakeholders are people who are affected by the decisions that the company makes. This can include not only the shareholders, but also the managers and other employees, people who reside in the area and customers of the company.

48) Which of the following is TRUE?

A) PACs are organized by SIGs
B) PACs and SIGs are organized by political parties
C) SIGs are organized by PACs
D) None of the above

The correct answer is A:) PACs are organized by SIGs. A special interest group (SIG) is any group which uses involvement in politics to further their beliefs and positions. Special interest groups do this by organizing political action committees (PACs).

49) Who has legal responsibility for a company's actions in a corporation?

    A) Chief Executive Officer
    B) Board of Directors
    C) Stakeholders
    D) Shareholders

The correct answer is B:) Board of Directors. The board of directors holds legal responsibility for the success of the firm and use of its assets, however they rarely control the day to day management of the firm. Rather, the board meets a few times a year and the managers and corporate officers oversee the actual day to day workings of the business.

50) Which of the following is the best example of point source pollution?

    A) An oil spill
    B) Fertilizer runoff
    C) Smoke stacks
    D) Smog

The correct answer is A:) An oil spill. Point-source pollution is a term relating to water pollution that has a specific and identifiable source. Answer C is specific and identifiable, but it is a form of air pollution.

51) Which of the following terms is most synonymous with philanthropy?

    A) Implied falsity
    B) Reciprocity
    C) Altruism
    D) Egoism

The correct answer is C:) Altruism. Altruism refers to placing the needs of another above oneself, such as through philanthropic acts. Reciprocity is the idea of treating others how you would wish to be treated.

52) Which of the following statements is TRUE?

   A) Trade secrets are new, non-obvious things that a company produces.
   B) Trademarks are information that a company wishes to keep private.
   C) Logos, jingles and brand names can all be examples of trademarks.
   D) Patents can be obtained for written materials.

The correct answer is C:) Logos, jingles and brand names can all be examples of trademarks. A trademark is anything which can be used to identify a specific product.

53) Which of the following is NOT a regulation for insiders trading stock?

   A) They must report stock trades within two business days of the trade
   B) They cannot buy and sell within a six month time frame
   C) They can only sell stock amounting to a 10 million dollar value at a time
   D) All of the above are regulations over insider trading

The correct answer is C:) They can only sell stock amounting to a 10 million dollar value at a time. Answers A and B are required for insiders legally trading stock.

54) Which of the following is NOT a conflict of interest?

   A) When a detective is involved with a case in which a close friend is a suspect.
   B) When a Congressman votes on a bill which benefits them financially.
   C) When a manager hires an employee who is also a close friend.
   D) All of the above are conflicts of interest.

The correct answer is D:) All of the above are conflicts of interest.

55) The fact that in many cases a company's worth is greater than the value of its tangible assets is referred to as

   A) Corporate value
   B) Social value
   C) Goodwill
   D) Equity

The correct answer is C:) Goodwill. There are intangible benefits which come as a result of having a good reputation and the intangible benefit that makes a company worth more when it is purchased by another company is referred to as goodwill.

56) Which of the following best describes rule utilitarianism?

   A) A person considers an action independently of a situation and determines whether it is more often moral or immoral to determine how to classify it in all situations.
   B) A person considers a situation and decides upon the easiest course of action.
   C) A person considers an action and determines whether it would end favorably for them.
   D) A person examines a situation, considers all possible actions they could take and decides which one would end most favorably for all involved.

The correct answer is A:) A person considers an action independently of a situation and determines whether it is more often moral or immoral to determine how to classify it in all situations.

57) A person is given the opportunity to volunteer at a local food bank. They consider the other things they could do at that time, such as cleaning and watching TV. They know that the work that they do could really benefit people at the food bank, whereas the other activities only benefit themselves. They decide that the service is the best decision for them. What type of ethical theory does their thought process and decision follow?

   A) Rule utilitarianism
   B) Act utilitarianism
   C) Deontological theory
   D) Ethical egoism

The correct answer is B:) Act utilitarianism. A person examines a situation, considers all possible actions they could take and decides which one would end most favorably for all involved.

58) Which of the following statements is TRUE?

   A) A grease payment involves relatively large amounts of money in comparison to bribes.
   B) A bribe involves extremely low level officials whereas a grease payment involves higher officials.
   C) A grease payment makes things that would normally occur happen at a faster rate.
   D) All of the above statements are incorrect.

The correct answer is C:) A grease payment makes things that would normally occur happen at a faster rate. In comparison, a bribe is an attempt to influence someone to act in a way that they normally would not. Therefore, bribes are illegal and grease payments are not.

59) If people object to something being built near their homes it is referred to as

   A) NIMBY
   B) NIMHS
   C) NIMN
   D) Residential objectivity

The correct answer is A:) NIMBY. This stands for "not in my backyard."

60) Which of the following statements is TRUE?

   A) Taxes have only positive impacts on the economy because they increase the amount of money that people spend which is healthy for the economy.
   B) Taxes are universally bad. They are unethical, unnecessary and harmful to efficient market operations.
   C) Taxes negatively impact efficient economic operations by driving a wedge between businesses and customers. However, they are often necessary.
   D) None of the above statements are true.

The correct answer is C:) Taxes negatively impact efficient economic operations by driving a wedge between businesses and customers. However, they are often necessary. Taxes make it so the price that customers pay is higher than the revenue that the company receives. The mismatch makes the economy run less efficiently.

61) Arable land is used for

   A) Farming
   B) Home development
   C) Business purposes
   D) Landfills

The correct answer is A:) Farming. Arable land is suitable for agricultural uses, i.e., farming.

62) Which of the following is NOT a concern relative to outsourcing?

   A) Language and cultural barriers
   B) Security
   C) Long distance management difficulties
   D) All of the above are concerns about outsourcing

The correct answer is D:) All of the above are concerns about outsourcing. Other problems that arise are fraud, the qualifications of employees and questions about the responsibility of a company that outsources for the actions of the company it hires.

63) Which of the following moral theories is NOT consequentialist?

   A) Teleology
   B) Act utilitarianism
   C) Egoism
   D) Kantian ethics

The correct answer is D:) Kantian ethics. Kantian ethics determines morality based on the morality of the action itself, not its consequences. It is deontological.

64) Which of the following statements is TRUE?

   A) Sustainable development requires that all people be prevented from over-using resources through government regulations.
   B) Sustainable development emphasizes the development of new and innovative technologies to reduce the overuse of natural resources.
   C) Sustainable development describes a tenuous state in which resource use is equal to consumption. While it can be sustained, it is not optimal.
   D) None of the above

The correct answer is B:) Sustainable development emphasizes the development of new and innovative technologies to reduce the overuse of natural resources. Through developing new technologies that are more energy efficient, people can continue to operate as they had previously without having to sacrifice the health of the environment.

65) Which of the following lists the four P's of advertising?

   A) Product, place, promotion, price
   B) Protocols, product, place, process
   C) Place, promotion, product, protocols
   D) None of the above

The correct answer is A:) Product, place, promotion, price. Each of these advertising factors has a number of ethical concerns involved with it.

66) Which of the following is NOT an unethical pricing strategy?

   A) Dumping
   B) Price cancellation
   C) Price discrimination
   D) Predatory pricing

The correct answer is B:) Price cancellation. Dumping, price discrimination and predatory pricing are all types of unethical pricing strategies.

67) Which of the following is NOT a rule for creating maxims under Kantian ethics?

    A) A maxim must be unconditional
    B) A maxim must be specific
    C) A maxim must be universal
    D) All of the above are rules for creating maxims

The correct answer is B:) The maxim must be specific. Maxims used in Kantian ethics are supposed to generalized.

68) Who is best known for creating the categorical imperative?

    A) Lawrence Kohlberg
    B) Jean Piaget
    C) Immanuel Kant
    D) John Stuart Mill

The correct answer is C:) Immanuel Kant. The categorical imperative is used to create the maxims which Kant believed morality should be determined using.

69) Which of the following statements would be most correct under a classical view of business?

    A) Government regulations are useful in helping the economy run more efficiently.
    B) Government regulations should be considered on a cost-benefit analysis.
    C) Government regulations are always detrimental because the economy is self-correcting.
    D) None of the above

The correct answer is C:) Government regulations are always detrimental because the economy is self-correcting.

70) Which act makes it illegal for U.S. citizens to participate in bribes?

    A) Sarbanes-Oxley Act
    B) Anti-Bribery Act
    C) Foreign Corrupt Practices Act
    D) Whistleblower Act

The correct answer is C:) Foreign Corrupt Practices Act. The Foreign Corrupt Practice Act also makes it illegal for a person of any nationality to further a bribe while on United States soil.

71) An employee of a donut shop does not steal donuts because they are afraid they would get fired if they did. Which of Kohlberg's stages are they in?

A) Stage 1
B) Stage 2
C) Stage 4
D) Stage 6

The correct answer is A:) Stage 1. In this stage a person is most concerned with avoiding punishment, such as getting fired.

72) Does the Foreign Corrupt Practices Act include grease payments?

A) Yes, grease payments are considered bribes and are therefore illegal under the FCPA.
B) Yes, grease payments are not considered bribes and are therefore illegal under the FCPA.
C) No, grease payments are considered bribes and are therefore not illegal under the FCPA.
D) No, grease payments are not considered bribes and are therefore not illegal under the FCPA.

The correct answer is D:) No, grease payments are not considered bribes and are therefore not illegal under the FCPA.

73) A stable state economy is in a state of

A) Sustainable development
B) Environmental renewal
C) Efficient energy consumption
D) Environmental equilibrium

The correct answer is D:) Environmental equilibrium.

74) Which of the following is NOT regulated by the FDA?

A) Blood transfusions
B) Illegal drugs
C) Vaccines
D) Cosmetics

The correct answer is B:) Illegal drugs. Illegal drugs are monitored by the Drug Enforcement Agency (DEA).

75) Which of the following is NOT a type of discrimination investigated by the EEOC?

   A) Gender
   B) Disability
   C) Education
   D) Religion

The correct answer is C:) Education. The EEOC investigates situations of discrimination based on age, gender, disability, race, color or religion.

76) The EEOC investigates violations of the

   A) WARN Act
   B) Kyoto Protocol
   C) Sarbanes-Oxley Act
   D) Civil Rights Act of 1964

The correct answer is D:) Civil Rights Act of 1964.

77) What does EEOC stand for?

   A) Equivalent Employment Opening Committee
   B) Equal Employment Opportunity Commission
   C) Equivalent Employment Opportunity Commission
   D) Equal Employment Opening Committee

The correct answer is B:) Equal Employment Opportunity Commission. The EEOC investigates discrimination based on age, gender, disability, race color and religion.

78) A business practices underhanded accounting practices to raise stock prices and make money. Which type of ethics does this fall under?

   A) Social
   B) Economical
   C) Legal
   D) Both A and C

The correct answer is B:) Economical. Economic ethics have to do with business and money related issues.

79) Which of the following describes in kind contributions?

   A) When a person contributes to a cause because they are in a good mood.
   B) When a person or company trades goods or services in place of money.
   C) When a company receives federal aid to implement a required environmental safety program.
   D) None of the above

The correct answer is B:) When a person or company trades goods or services in place of money. For example, donating lumber to an organization which builds homes for homeless people.

80) Which of the following is NOT a benefit which can come to companies as a result of sustainable business practices?

   A) Assurance of the ability to operate in the future
   B) Lower energy costs and waste disposal costs in the long run
   C) Better relations with stakeholders
   D) All of the above are possible benefits

The correct answer is D:) All of the above are possible benefits. There are many benefits which come to companies as a result of safe and sustainable practices, of which answers A, B and C are all examples.

81) What is the responsibility of the FDA?

   A) To regulate the marketing and sale of potentially dangerous products.
   B) To create regulations which limit the ability of grocery stores to advertise.
   C) To create equal trade of agricultural products among all nations.
   D) To ensure and protect public health and safety.

The correct answer is D:) To ensure and protect public health and safety. The FDA works to ensure that products are safe, sanitary and properly labeled.

82) Which of the following is regulated by the FDA?

   A) Toys and appliances
   B) Alcohol
   C) Radioactive products
   D) Advertisement

The correct answer is C:) Radioactive products. Advertisement of most products is not regulated by the FDA, and neither are toys, appliances or alcohol. However, radioactive products are regulated by the FDA because they are a threat to public safety.

83) The Kimberley Process Certification Scheme was created to stop the circulation of what?

   A) Rough diamonds
   B) Cut diamonds
   C) Conflict diamonds
   D) Uncertified diamonds

The correct answer is C:) Conflict diamonds. Conflict diamonds are also called war diamonds or blood diamonds.

84) Which of the following is NOT an example of an in kind contribution?

   A) Donating lumber to an organization which builds homes for homeless people.
   B) Donating money to a humanitarian organization for the purchase of blankets.
   C) When two companies or people exchange services in place of paying each other.
   D) A broadcasting company airing a message for free instead of donating to a political campaign.

The correct answer is B:) Donating money to a humanitarian organization for the purchase of blankets. In kind contributions are when a person or company trades goods or services in place of money. In this example money is donated.

85) The origins of the FDA can be traced to which of the following Acts?

   A) Pure Food and Drug Act
   B) Sarbanes-Oxley Act
   C) Sanitary Production Act
   D) Corporate Social Responsibilities Act

The correct answer is A:) Pure Food and Drug Act. The Pure Food and Drug Act was passed in 1906 to force food producing industries to practice sanitation.

86) Which of the following is NOT a right outlined in the Privacy Act of 1974?

   A) A person has the right to request corrections to documents about them that are incomplete or incorrect.
   B) The act prevents unauthorized disclosure of information from systems of records to other people or government agencies.
   C) A person has the right to remove documents about themselves from government records.
   D) A person has the right to know of government records kept about them (in systems of records).

The correct answer is C:) A person has the right to remove documents about themselves from government records. A, B and D all correctly describe rights of the Privacy Act, however the act does not give a person the right to remove documents about themselves.

87) Which of the following is NOT a way in which businesses are regulated?

   A) Protection of consumers
   B) Regulation of competition
   C) Ensure safety and equality
   D) All of the above are ways in which businesses are regulated

The correct answer is D:) All of the above are ways in which businesses are regulated. Business can regulated through actual laws (as in the three areas above) and through their own ethical codes.

88) Which of the following is NOT a way that governments can influence businesses?

   A) Through PACs
   B) Taxes
   C) Procompetitive laws
   D) Tariffs

The correct answer is A:) Through PACs. PACs, or Political Action Committees are groups that work to campaign for a particular candidate. It is therefore a way that businesses can influence politics, not the other way around.

89) OSHA was created to do which of the following?

   A) Protect consumers' rights
   B) Ensure worker safety
   C) Ensure equality in the workplace
   D) Protect the market against monopolies

The correct answer is B:) Ensure worker safety. OSHA is the Occupational Safety and Health Administration and works to enforce safety laws and improve safety in the workplace.

90) A virus is

   A) A piece of software which is able to delete information or damage programs on a computer.
   B) A piece of code which spreads from computer to computer and can disrupt computer functions.
   C) A piece of software which can send information over the internet to allow personalization.
   D) A type of message which is sent indiscriminately to a large number of people over the internet.

The correct answer is B:) A piece of code which spreads from computer to computer and can disrupt computer functions. For example, viruses can delete information, slow the computer down or damage software.

91) What are conflict diamonds?

   A) Diamonds which are sold with the purpose of funding insurrection or war.
   B) Diamonds which different companies start a war over control for.
   C) Diamonds for which the country of origin is not known.
   D) None of the above

The correct answer is A:) Diamonds which are sold with the purpose of funding insurrection or war. For this reason they are also called war diamonds or blood diamonds.

92) Which of the following is NOT an agency responsible for protecting worker's health?

   A) OSHA
   B) EPA
   C) KPCS
   D) All of the above are responsible for protecting workers health

The correct answer is C:) KPCS. The Kimberly Protocol Certification Scheme (KPCS) works to reduce the circulation of conflict diamonds. OSHA and the EPA are responsible for protecting worker's health.

93) Protections for workers from workplace hazards are regulated and mandated by which agency?

   A) OSHA
   B) EPA
   C) KPCS
   D) Labor unions

The correct answer is A:) OSHA. OSHA stands for the Occupational Safety and Health Administration.

94) Which of the following BEST describes affirmative action?

   A) Any program at a university which aims at increasing the presence of minority groups.
   B) A set of quotas that must be met by universities in admitting people of minority races.
   C) Any program which seeks to reverse the effects of any form of discrimination.
   D) A requirement under the ADA which forces employers to favor disabled workers.

The correct answer is C:) Any program which seeks to reverse the effects of any form of discrimination. The term affirmative action is most often used in terms of minority groups, though it technically applies to all forms of discrimination.

95) Which of the following statements is TRUE?

   A) In almost every case, autocratic leadership has a negative impact on the workplace and should be substituted with either delegative or democratic styles.
   B) Although both compliance and values oriented ethical programs improve short run ethical practices in a workplace, in the long run values oriented programs show negative effects.
   C) The shareholder model of corporate governance is the precursor to the stakeholder model.
   D) An effective leader should be able to switch between transformational and transactional leadership styles.

The correct answer is D:) An effective leader should be able to switch between transformational and transactional leadership styles. Neither transformational nor transactional leadership is considered to be outright better than the alternative, and most people believe that a truly effective leader should be able to use both styles as the situation may demand.

96) Some people believe that women earn less than men because female held jobs have been historically devalued, and that women should be given equal pay for equal work. This belief is called

   A) Comparable worth
   B) Affirmative action
   C) Glass ceiling
   D) Absenteeism

The correct answer is A:) Comparable worth. The idea is that jobs typically held by women receive lower pay on average than jobs typically held by men. Advocates of comparable worth work to ensure that jobs typically held by women that require the same amount of effort and risk as jobs typically held by men (even though they may not be similar) receive equal pay.

97) Which of the following statements best describes the difference between corporate intelligence and corporate espionage?

   A) There is no difference between corporate intelligence and corporate espionage. They are two terms for the same thing.
   B) Both are illegal forms of information gathering. Corporate espionage focuses on the social engineering and more personal aspect of gathering information and corporate intelligence involves hacking and other software based methods of information gathering.
   C) Corporate espionage involves legally gathering information about a company and corporate intelligence involves illegally gathering information about a company.
   D) Corporate intelligence involves legally gathering information about a company and corporate espionage involves illegally gathering information about a company.

The correct answer is D:) Corporate intelligence involves legally gathering information about a company and corporate espionage involves illegally gathering information about a company.

98) If a person were to sue a company for not fulfilling a contractual obligation, it would be a

   A) Civil rights case
   B) Civil case
   C) Criminal case
   D) Affirmative action case

The correct answer is B:) Civil case. In civil cases on party (the person) sues another party (the company) because they feel like their rights have been violated, in this case because the company did not fulfill their obligations.

99) Which of the following statements is FALSE?

   A) Criminal laws are enforced by the government.
   B) The only ethical regulations businesses follow are mandated by the government.
   C) The ADA requires that "reasonable accommodation" be given to disabled employees.
   D) All of the above are true statements.

The correct answer is B:) The only ethical regulations businesses follow are mandated by the government. This is incorrect because many businesses have their own ethical standards and ethics programs. Also, many are governed by core practices which are ethical codes that are inherent within the business (for example, quality checks on products).

100) The perceived "us" versus "them" mentality that emerges when doing business with different cultures is referred to as

   A) Egoistic perception
   B) Self reference criterion
   C) Cultural displacement
   D) Relativism

The correct answer is B:) Self reference criterion.

101) An ombudsman is

   A) A type of program that is used in cost-benefit analysis to help companies make decisions.
   B) A leader in a movement to establish a union in a workplace.
   C) An intermediary who investigates complaints against a group.
   D) None of the above

The correct answer is C:) An intermediary who investigates complaints against a group. An ombudsman is hired by the group about which they investigate complaints and can be very helpful in increasing workplace efficiency.

102) Which of the following does not relate in some manner to international trade?

   A) Kyoto Protocol
   B) NAFTA
   C) EEOC
   D) WTO

The correct answer is C:) EEOC. The EEOC (Equal Employment Opportunities Commission) has to do with employment in the United States whereas NAFTA (North American Free Trade Agreement), WTO (World Trade Organization) and the Kyoto Protocol all relate to trade on a multinational level.

103) Which of the following did the Bipartisan Campaign Reform Act NOT do?

   A) Prohibited non-partisan ads funded by corporations or unions near elections.
   B) Stated that contributions exceeding $10,000 must be disclosed.
   C) Raised the amount of hard money that could be raised.
   D) The act did all of the above.

The correct answer is D:) The act did all of the above.

104) Oversight refers to

   A) Finding ways to ensure that the decisions of managers and employees are aligned with the ethical principles and goals of the company.
   B) Finding ways to eliminate the opportunities for employees to act unethically.
   C) The ability of the company to consider decisions and improve where necessary.
   D) An ineffective leadership style in which leaders are constantly checking on the performance of employees.

The correct answer is B:) Finding ways to eliminate the opportunities for employees to act unethically. Specifically, oversight refers to creating a set of checks and balances which prevent employees from making unethical decisions.

105) The FTC was created to monitor which type of regulation?

   A) Laws regulating competition
   B) Laws regulating equality and safety
   C) Laws regulating consumer protection
   D) None of the above

The correct answer is C:) Laws regulating consumer protection. More specifically, the FTC's Bureau of Consumer Protection more specifically works to protect consumers from unfair business practices by regulating advertising and marketing, finances and protecting privacy.

106) Which of the following is NOT a type of imperative considered under Kantian ethics?

   A) Categorical imperative
   B) Universal imperative
   C) Hypothetical imperative
   D) Practical imperative

The correct answer is B:) Universal imperative. Universality is a condition of a good maxim, however Kantian ethics does not discuss an universal imperative.

107) Fast food places do not pay their workers less than minimum wage because it is against the law. Which of Kohlberg's stages does this describe?

A) Stage 1
B) Stage 2
C) Stage 3
D) Stage 4

The correct answer is D:) Stage 4. In Stage 4, people are motivated primarily by authority, such as the law.

108) Which of the following is more typical of a values oriented ethical program than a compliance oriented ethics program?

A) A strong focus on developing core values
B) Formal descriptions of ethical standards
C) Specific punishments tied to ethical performance
D) None of the above

The correct answer is A:) A strong focus on developing core values. A values oriented program would still set forth some standards and punishments for obvious ethical violations, but they focus more on ensuring that employees adhere to a set of core values.

109) Utilitarianism is a type of

A) Consequentialism
B) Relativism
C) Deontological ethics
D) Egoism

The correct answer is A:) Consequentialism. Utilitarianism considers the consequences of an action and the extent to which they benefit society in determining morality, therefore it is consequential.

110) Which of the following is the stakeholder model of corporate governance?

   A) A manager must focus solely on improving the returns to stockholders and pleasing them.
   B) A manager must ensure that workplace decisions are aligned with the ethical principles and goals of the company.
   C) A manager must focus specifically on improving customer relations because customers are the most important stakeholders.
   D) A manager must consider which group of stakeholders is most important to please and then work towards developing positive long term relationships with that group.

The correct answer is D:) A manager must consider which group of stakeholders is most important to please and then work towards developing positive long term relationships with that group.

111) A lawyer knows that their client is guilty, but defends them anyways. This falls under which type of ethics?

   A) Social
   B) Economical
   C) Legal
   D) Both B and C

The correct answer is C:) Legal. Legal ethics has to do with the actions of lawyers.

112) A cookie

   A) Infects the computer so that black patches appear across the screen.
   B) Allows an origin site to send information to a computer's browser.
   C) Is a type of software used to send out large amounts of email indiscriminately.
   D) All of the above

The correct answer is B:) Allows an origin site to send information to a computer's browser. This way web sites can be personalized and shopping carts can "hold" items in your cart from visit to visit.

113) Which of the following statements is FALSE?

   A) Random drug testing of employees is allowed in all cases.
   B) An employer does not have the right to demand that an employee take a lie detector test.
   C) Employers should not ask employees about off duty behaviors unless they are damaging to the company.
   D) None of the above

The correct answer is A:) Random drug testing of employees is allowed in all cases. Although in some professions (those which are deemed to have safety concerns involved) random drug testing is allowed, in others, drug testing is allowed only upon application or with reasonable cause.

114) Which of the following is NOT true of NAFTA?

   A) NAFTA stands for North American Free Trade Agreement.
   B) As a part of NAFTA, Canada and the United States agree to help Mexico in trade matters.
   C) NAFTA works to lower trade barriers between the United States, Canada and Mexico.
   D) NAFTA is responsible for dealing with trade disputes between the United States, Canada and Mexico.

The correct answer is B:) As a part of NAFTA, Canada and the United States agree to help Mexico in trade matters. Answers A, C and D all describe responsibilities of NAFTA.

115) Which of the following types of contributions to a political campaign have donation limits imposed by law?

   A) Soft money
   B) Foreign currency
   C) Hard money
   D) All of the above

The correct answer is C:) Hard money. Hard money is donated to a specific candidate for the purpose of campaigning and there are legal limits to the amount of hard money which a person or business can donate to a campaign.

116) Which of the following theories claims that a person should only act in their own best interest?

A) Consequentialism
B) Kantian ethics
C) Ethical egoism
D) Ethical relativism

The correct answer is C:) Ethical egoism. In other words, the theory states that if it benefits the person then it is the right thing for them to do.

117) Lobbying is

A) Raising large amounts of money for a certain political candidate.
B) Meeting with senators, representatives, staff members or other important people to persuade them to vote how you wish them to.
C) Running ads that promote a certain political candidate or viewpoint.
D) None of the above

The correct answer is B:) Meeting with senators, representatives, staff members or other important people to persuade them to vote how you wish them to.

118) Which of the following theories claims that ethical beliefs are determined by the society in which one lives?

A) Teleological ethics
B) Ethical relativism
C) Consequentialism
D) Ethical egoism

The correct answer is B:) Ethical relativism. In other words, the theory states that there really is no universal set of morals because they are determined by the state and opinion of the society in which one lives.

119) Which of the following aids employers in keeping information private?

A) False Claims Act
B) NDAs
C) Civil Rights Act
D) Fair Labor Standards Act

The correct answer is B:) NDAs. This stands for Non-Disclosure Agreements. They are legally binding and specify who isn't allowed to share what information and for how long.

120) Why did the Supreme Court rule in favor of Wal-Mart in the case of Dukes vs Wal-Mart?

   A) Because Dukes did not actually have any evidence showing discrimination.
   B) Because Dukes could not prove that all women employees faced discriminatory practices.
   C) Because Dukes consistently had negative performance reviews.
   D) None of the above

The correct answer is B:) Because Dukes could not prove that all women employees faced discriminatory practices. Dukes claimed to represent 1.6 million female employees of Wal-Mart.

121) Which of the following is a way in which government interventions in the economy can be beneficial to consumers?

   A) Product safety regulations
   B) Import tariffs
   C) Taxes
   D) Both A and B

The correct answer is D:) Both A and B. Taxes make the economy operate less efficiently. Product safety regulations are beneficial to consumers by making products safer. Tariffs are not beneficial to consumers because it raises the price of imported goods allowing U.S. producers to charge more.

122) Hard money is

   A) Donated to political parties
   B) Donated to a candidate's campaign
   C) Donated specifically by a business
   D) All of the above

The correct answer is B:) Donated to a candidate's campaign. Hard money is donated to a specific candidate for the purpose of campaigning and there are legal limits to the amount of hard money which a person or business can donate to a campaign.

123) What is the purpose of the WARN Act?

   A) It requires employers to give workers notice before mass layoffs so that they can prepare.
   B) To stop the circulation of conflict diamonds by cautioning sellers that diamonds that are mined in areas where there are wars will not be purchased.
   C) To restore stakeholder confidence in securities markets by requiring that companies inform the public of their financial situation through general purpose financial statements.
   D) To lower greenhouse gas emissions. The act begins by acknowledging that there are serious possible consequences to not doing so.

The correct answer is A:) It requires employers to give workers notice before mass layoffs so that they can prepare. WARN stands for Workers Adjustment and Retraining Notification Act.

124) Which of the following is NOT true of the WTO?

   A) The World Trade Organization deals with trade on a global level.
   B) One responsibility of the WTO is to help developing countries in trade matters.
   C) The WTO is responsible for overseeing trade disputes among its member countries.
   D) The WTO is governed by a conference of Secretariats with one Secretariat from each country.

The correct answer is D:) The WTO is governed by a conference of Secretariats with one Secretariat from each country. The WTO is governed via a Ministerial conference held every two years. NAFTA is governed by Secretariats.

125) How many days of notice does the WARN Act require employers to give employees?

   A) 30 days
   B) 60 days
   C) 90 days
   D) 100 days

The correct answer is B:) 60 days. This allows the workers time to adjust their lives accordingly to an upcoming mass layoff or closure.

126) Which of the following would NOT be illegal under the Foreign Corrupt Practices Act?

   A) If a company pays a low level official to ensure that their employees receive work visas more quickly than normal.
   B) If a company compensates an official in return for giving them preferential treatment in business contracts.
   C) If a company pays a building inspector to overlook certain regulations when considering whether their offices are built in line with safety regulations.
   D) All of the above are illegal under the Foreign Corrupt Practices Act.

The correct answer is A:) If a company pays a low level official to ensure that their employees receive work visas more quickly than normal. This would be a grease payment, which is not considered illegal under the Foreign Corrupt Practices Act.

127) The Dukes vs. Wal-Mart case involves which issue?

   A) Illegal accounting practices
   B) Invasion of employee privacy
   C) Violation of an NDA
   D) Sexual discrimination

The correct answer is D:) Sexual discrimination. Dukes claimed that she was passed over for training that would have allowed her to advance to a salaried position because she was a woman.

128) In the case of Watson vs. Fort Worth Bank and Trust the court ruled that

   A) It is always discriminatory for employers to hire on a basis of only subjective considerations.
   B) Employers always have the right to use whatever hiring practices they want, even if they may be inherently discriminatory.
   C) Employers may use subjective considerations for hiring as long as they do not produce a discriminatory environment.
   D) None of the above

The correct answer is C:) Employers may use subjective considerations for hiring as long as they do not produce a discriminatory environment. Although in Watson's case the court did not find that there was significant evidence that this was the case.

129) Which of the following is NOT true of sexual harassment?

   A) The claimant must be able to prove a hostile work environment was created.
   B) Sexual harassment is any repeated, unwanted behavior of a sexual nature.
   C) Sexual harassment can apply to physical actions, words, images and written material.
   D) The primary factor in sexual harassment cases is the intent of the action.

The correct answer is D:) The primary factor in sexual harassment cases is the intent of the action. On the contrary, the primary factor is the effect of the action, or how it is perceived, not the intent.

130) Which of the following cases established that it was how actions were interpreted that matter in sexual harassment cases?

   A) Watson vs. Fort Worth Bank and Trust
   B) Harris vs. Forklift Systems, Inc.
   C) Dukes vs. Wal-Mart
   D) Roe vs. Wade

The correct answer is B:) Harris vs. Forklift Systems, Inc. It was determined that because a reasonable person would have been offended by the remarks made and would have interpreted them negatively it was a case of sexual harassment.

131) Which of the following correctly describes the legality of camera surveillance methods in a workplace?

   A) All types of visual and audio surveillance are allowable in workplaces.
   B) Although audio surveillance is essentially unrestricted, there are limits to an employer's use of video surveillance.
   C) Although video surveillance is essentially unrestricted, there are limits to an employer's use of audio surveillance.
   D) No type of visual or audio surveillance is allowable in workplaces.

The correct answer is C:) Although video surveillance is essentially unrestricted, there are limits to an employer's use of audio surveillance.

132) A grease payment can also be called a

    A) Rush payment
    B) Facilitating payment
    C) Noisy withdrawal
    D) Bribe

The correct answer is B:) Facilitating payment. A grease payment is a bribe made to make something happen faster than it normally would.

133) Which of the following would NOT be addressed in a Non-Disclosure Agreement?

    A) The time period in which the person may not discuss the confidential information
    B) Descriptions of the parties involved in the NDA
    C) Descriptions of the information which is to remain confidential
    D) All of the above would be addressed in an NDA

The correct answer is D:) All of the above would be addressed in an NDA.

134) What is the purpose of the Kyoto Protocol?

    A) It requires employers to give workers notice before mass layoffs so that they can prepare.
    B) To stop the circulation of conflict diamonds.
    C) To restore stakeholder confidence in securities markets.
    D) To lower greenhouse gas emissions.

The correct answer is D:) To lower greenhouse gas emissions. The protocol aimed at lowering worldwide emissions by 5.2%, using 1990 as the benchmark year.

135) Ergonomics is

   A) The study of designing more comfortably or easily used equipment.
   B) When a person is in a position to exploit their power for their own benefit.
   C) A moral theory which claims that the morality of an action is determined by the morality of the action itself – regardless of the consequence.
   D) When a lawyer withdraws legal representation for their client and notifies the proper authorities.

The correct answer is A:) The study of designing more comfortably or easily used equipment. With ergonomics, a person's working environment is altered to suit them instead of the person having to adapt to their environment.

136) In which of the following situations would an NDA NOT be used?

   A) When a potential investor wants access to proprietary information.
   B) When two companies are working together to develop a new product.
   C) When a company developing cutting edge technology hires a new employee.
   D) An NDA would be appropriate in all of the above situations.

The correct answer is D:) An NDA would be appropriate in all of the above situations. In each case described there will be information disclosed that the companies would want (and have a right) to keep confidential.

137) Karen Silkwood is associated with which of the following?

   A) Kerr-McGee
   B) OSHA
   C) KPCS
   D) EEOC

The correct answer is A:) Kerr-McGee. Karen Silkwood was an employee of a plant, Kerr-McGee, which produced plutonium pellets to fuel nuclear reactors. She died suspiciously after investigating the plant's inadequate safety measures.

138) Which of the following is NOT illegal?

   A) Discrimination in general
   B) Statistical discrimination
   C) Unintentional discrimination
   D) Neither B nor C

The correct answer is D:) Neither B nor C. Statistical discrimination, also known as unintentional discrimination, is when numerically it appears that a certain group is being discriminated against, although it is a result of outside factors and not discrimination. It is therefore not illegal.

139) The term glass ceiling relates to which of the following employer-employee relations issues?

   A) Wages
   B) Confidentiality
   C) Discrimination
   D) Labor union relations

The correct answer is C:) Discrimination. A glass ceiling is describes an invisible barrier to the advancement of a group. It is sometimes used to describe the fact that there are discriminatory practices facing certain groups.

140) Which of the following does NOT focus on increasing the ethical awareness of employees and strengthening the ethical culture of a workplace?

   A) Transformational leadership
   B) Democratic leadership style
   C) Values oriented ethical programs
   D) All of the above focus on increasing ethical standards of employees

The correct answer is B:) Democratic leadership style. The democratic leadership style is a leadership style which involves collaboration and communication among leaders and workers. It's not really involved with the ethical awareness of employees.

141) Which of the following is NOT a part of the corporate social responsibility pyramid?

A) Legal
B) Economic
C) Ethical
D) Environmental justice

The correct answer is D:) Environmental justice. The four parts of the corporate social responsibility pyramid are: legal, economic, ethical and philanthropic.

142) Which of the following is NOT an illegal basis of discrimination?

A) Race
B) Age
C) Education
D) Gender

The correct answer is C:) Education. Education relates to job qualifications and therefore it is not illegal to consider it when dealing with hiring and firing practices.

143) Which of the following is NOT a guideline set forth by the Supreme Court to be used in creating affirmative action programs?

A) The program should apply only to qualified candidates.
B) There must be a strong demonstrable need for the program.
C) The program should be temporary and flexible.
D) All of the above are correct guidelines.

The correct answer is D:) All of the above are correct guidelines. It is important to be careful when designing affirmative action programs to avoid creating a status of reverse-discrimination. Therefore the program should fulfill a demonstrated need, benefit only qualified candidates and should not be strict and rigidly defined.

144) Which of the following is NOT legally required in management relations with labor unions?

A) That management bargain in good faith with labor unions.
B) That management agrees to terms set forth by labor unions.
C) That management agrees to negotiate with labor unions.
D) That management addresses certain subjects such as wages and hours in negotiations with labor union representatives.

The correct answer is B:) That management agrees to terms set forth by labor unions. Although A, C and D are required of management, they do not have to agree to the terms set forth by labor unions.

145) Which of the following statements BEST describes attitudes toward outsourcing?

A) It is universally accepted that outsourcing is an unethical practice that doesn't provide benefits to anyone.
B) Outsourcing is often criticized, however it can have many economic benefits because it allows companies to produce at a lower cost.
C) Outsourcing is a highly supported practice and most people wish to see more of it because it reduces ethical concerns that face businesses.
D) All of the above

The correct answer is B:) Outsourcing is often criticized, however it can have many economic benefits because it allows companies to produce at a lower cost. Although outsourcing can reduce production costs for a business (thus increasing returns to stockholders and reducing the end price to consumers) it is often criticized for moving jobs away from locals. It also brings a whole new set of difficult economic concerns.

146) The Fair Labor Standards Act

A) Prohibits minimum wages that are too high.
B) Prohibits unethical dual relationships that alter the terms of employment for employees.
C) Sets forth standards for management in relations with labor unions.
D) Makes discrimination on a basis of prior employment illegal.

The correct answer is C:) Sets forth standards for management in relations with labor unions. The FLSR states that management must negotiate with labor union representatives, negotiate in good faith and address topics such as employment conditions, wages and hours.

147) Which of the following BEST describes the "old" social contract?

   A) Workers could expect good benefits in any job they chose.
   B) If workers were loyal, punctual and at least decently efficient they could expect to keep their jobs and perhaps even advance over time.
   C) Workers had no expectations of their work environments. They could be fired or laid off at any time.
   D) Employees must work to the best of their ability, increase their knowledge, improve over time and be loyal and ethical in their work to keep their jobs.

The correct answer is B:) If workers were loyal, punctual and at least decently efficient they could expect to keep their jobs and perhaps even advance over time.

148) Implied falsity is

   A) Advertising which involves unreasonable and purposefully misleading claims
   B) Advertising which involves technically true claims which are misleading by nature
   C) Advertising which is not true in any sense
   D) None of the above

The correct answer is B:) Advertising which involves technically true claims which are misleading by nature.

149) What type of information is compiled to answer a specific question?

   A) Ad hoc
   B) Proprietary information
   C) Stakeholder information
   D) Trade secrets

The correct answer is A:) Ad hoc. Ad hoc is a Latin term which literally means "for this."

150) Which of the following is NOT a result of a shift to the "new" social contract?

A) Downsizing
B) Higher expectations of workers
C) Pay raises
D) All of the above are results of a "new" social contract.

The correct answer is C:) Pay raises. The "new" social contract of the workplace requires an employee to work to the best of their ability, increase their knowledge, improve over time and be loyal and ethical in their work. Often downsizing occurs because certain positions are unnecessary.

151) The intent of the Sarbanes-Oxley Act was to

A) Help companies be better able to deal with the ethical problems raised by increased technology.
B) Restore stakeholder confidence in the securities market after a series of scandals in the early 2000s.
C) Create a commission that would monitor the accounting records of major businesses.
D) Scare businesses into conforming with the GAAP standards in their accounting practices.

The correct answer is B:) Restore stakeholder confidence in the securities market after a series of scandals in the early 2000s.

152) Which of the following statements is NOT true?

A) Outsourcing is when a company moves part of its business to another location.
B) Outsourcing can help companies save money and keep prices down.
C) Outsourcing is unanimously agreed to be a beneficial process.
D) All of the above statements are true.

The correct answer is C:) Outsourcing is unanimously agreed to be a beneficial process. There are positive and negative aspects of outsourcing.

153) Which of the following is NOT a form of marketing fraud?

- A) Predatory pricing
- B) Misstating financial statements
- C) Price discrimination
- D) Untruthful advertising

The correct answer is B:) Misstating financial statements. Altering or incorrectly reporting financial statements would be a form of accounting fraud, not a form of marketing fraud. Predatory pricing, price discrimination and untruthful advertising are all marketing schemes.

154) Which of the following is NOT a legal way for employers to monitor employees?

- A) Placing video cameras in workplaces
- B) Enquiring about off duty activities
- C) Viewing messages sent over company networks
- D) Listening to phone conversations on company lines

The correct answer is B:) Enquiring about off duty activities. Employers have very few rights over their employee's off duty actions unless they can show that those actions are impairing their ability to do their job.

155) The Tyco scandal is associated with which of the following Acts?

- A) WARN
- B) Sarbanes-Oxley Act
- C) Foreign Corrupt Practices Act
- D) Privacy Act

The correct answer is B:) Sarbanes-Oxley Act. Tyco executives used the company's employee loan program to take extravagant vacations and give themselves bonuses without ever paying back the money. It was one of the scandals which spurred the Sarbanes-Oxley Act.

156) Corporate governance is

   A) A policy which demands that a company "gives back" to the communities in which it operates.
   B) The responsibility of a business to ensure maximum returns to its investors.
   C) A system of accountability, oversight and control within the company.
   D) The consideration of companies about the well-being of society when they make business decisions.

The correct answer is C:) A system of accountability, oversight and control within the company.

157) Which of the following is NOT a component of the SA8000 certification?

   A) Forced labor
   B) Wages
   C) Unions
   D) Proprietary information

The correct answer is D:) Proprietary information. The SA8000 certification process includes eight areas which are child labour, forced labour, health and safety, free association and collective bargaining, discrimination, disciplinary practices, working hours and compensation.

158) An employer who posted a list of weekly responsibilities for employees to fulfill would best be described as following which leadership style?

   A) Transformational
   B) Democratic
   C) Authoritative
   D) Free reign

The correct answer is C:) Authoritative. The authoritative, or autocratic, leadership style involves a leader who makes decisions and tells employees what their responsibilities are.

159) Which of the following is associated with protecting employee's rights?

   A) EPPA
   B) EPA
   C) KPCS
   D) All of the above

The correct answer is A:) EPPA. The Employee Polygraph Protection Act protects employees from having to take lie detector tests, except in a few circumstances such as government employees.

160) Ronald Reagan's Executive Order 12564 focused on

   A) Forced labor
   B) Wages
   C) Drug testing
   D) Proprietary information

The correct answer is C:) Drug testing.

161) Who created the corporate social responsibility pyramid?

   A) David Hume
   B) Immanuel Kant
   C) Abraham Maslow
   D) Archie Carroll

The correct answer is D:) Archie Carroll.

162) The term quid pro quo relates to which of the following issues?

   A) Discrimination
   B) Sexual harassment
   C) Wages
   D) Environmental justice

The correct answer is B:) Sexual harassment.

163) The _____ was created under the Marrakesh Agreement in January of 1995 with the express purpose to regulate international trade in areas such as goods, intellectual property, and services.

   A) World Trade Center
   B) World Trade Organization
   C) World Trade Conglomerate
   D) World Trade Federation

The correct answer is B:) World Trade Organization.

164) Commonly referred to as a confidentiality agreement, a _____ is a legal document between two or more parties that outlines the sharing of sensitive information and restricts access to individuals not part of the agreement.

   A) Disclosure agreement
   B) Exclusive agreement
   C) Non-inclusive agreement
   D) Non-disclosure agreement

The correct answer is D:) Non-disclosure agreement.

165) Latin for "something for something," _____ is the term used to indicate that a good or service has been traded for something of value.

   A) Felix culpa
   B) Carpe diem
   C) Quid pro quo
   D) Bona fide

The correct answer is C:) Quid pro quo.

166) A _____ allows a lawyer to sever a client relationship when the lawyer knows, or it is apparent that, an ethical breach could occur or has occurred due to client interactions. In this particular instance, a lawyer would then be allowed to disclose protected client information.

   A) Noisy withdrawal
   B) Normal withdrawal
   C) Friendly withdrawal
   D) Contentious withdrawal

The correct answer is A:) Noisy withdrawal.

167) _____ was a 2011 Supreme Court case that centered around alleged gender discrimination in promotion and pay practices at Walmart stores.

   A) Walmart vs. Jones
   B) Walmart vs. Rogers
   C) Walmart vs. Stanley
   D) Walmart vs. Dukes

The correct answer is D:) Walmart vs. Dukes.

168) In _____, a 1993 unanimous Supreme Court decision determined a more specific definition of what constituted an abusive and hostile work environment under Title VII of the Civil Rights Act of 1964. Specifically, to determine whether a work environment qualifies as either requires consideration of all relevant circumstances.

   A) Walmart vs. Forklift Systems, Inc.
   B) Harris vs. Forklift Systems, Inc.
   C) Walmart vs. Dukes
   D) Harris vs. Dukes

The correct answer is B:) Harris vs. Forklift Systems, Inc.

169) The _____ provides the federal government the framework to protect trade and commerce against monopolies and unlawful business restraints.

   A) Sherman Antitrust Act of 1980
   B) CAN-SPAM Act of 2003
   C) Clayton Act of 1914
   D) Federal Trade Commission Act of 1914

The correct answer is A:) Sherman Antitrust Act of 1980. The other answers are various other federal antitrust or business laws.

170) In 2000, the _____ was established to prevent conflict diamonds from entering the mainstream diamond market by verifying diamond purchases were not being used to finance rebel activities.

   A) Reginald Process
   B) Elizabeth Process
   C) Kimberley Process
   D) Edward Process

The correct answer is C:) Kimberley Process.

171) In an effort to combat global warming, the _____ was created to commit countries to reducing greenhouse gas emissions on the basis that human-made CO_2 emissions were the leading cause in rising levels.

   A) Tokyo Protocol
   B) Nagasaki Protocol
   C) Osaka Protocol
   D) Kyoto Protocol

The correct answer is D:) Kyoto Protocol. Created in 1997 in Japan, the Kyoto Protocol became effective on 2005 and was meant to extend upon the 1992 United Nations Framework Convention on Climate Change (UNFCCC).

172) A _____ or bribe is a monetary payment made to a specific individual or government official to expedite a business transaction, process, or shipment.

   A) Oil payment
   B) Pam payment
   C) Crisco payment
   D) Grease payment

The correct answer is D:) Grease payment.

Test Taking Strategies

Here are some test-taking strategies that are specific to this test and to other DSST tests in general:

- Keep your eyes on the time. Pay attention to how much time you have left.
- Read the entire question and read all the answers. Many questions are not as hard to answer as they may seem. Sometimes, a difficult sounding question really only is asking you how to read an accompanying chart. Chart and graph questions are on most DANTES/DSST tests and should be an easy free point.
- If you don't know the answer immediately, the new computer-based testing lets you mark questions and come back to them later if you have time.
- Read the wording carefully. Some words can give you hints to the right answer. There are no exceptions to an answer when there are words in the question such as always, all or none. If one of the answer choices includes most or some of the right answers, but not all, then that is not the answer. Here is an example:

    The primary colors include all of the following:
    A) Red, Yellow, Blue, Green
    B) Red, Green, Yellow
    C) Red, Orange, Yellow
    D) Red, Yellow, Blue

    Although item A includes all the right answers, it also includes an incorrect answer, making it incorrect. If you didn't read it carefully, were in a hurry, or didn't know the material well, you might fall for this.

- Make a guess on a question that you do not know the answer to. There is no penalty for an incorrect answer. Eliminate the answer choices that you know are incorrect. For example, this will let your guess be a 1 in 3 chance instead.

What Your Score Means

Based on your score, you may, or may not, qualify for credit at your specific institution. The current ACE recommended score for this exam is 400. Your school may require a higher or lower score to receive credit. To find out what score you need for credit, you need to get that information from your school's website or academic advisor.

You lose no points for incorrect questions so make sure you answer each question. If you don't know, make an educated guess. On this particular test, you must answer 100 questions in 90 minutes.

Test Preparation

How much you need to study depends on your knowledge of a subject area. If you are interested in literature, took it in school, or enjoy reading then your study and preparation for the literature or humanities test will not need to be as intensive as that of someone who is new to literature.

This book is much different than the regular CLEP study guides. This book actually teaches you the information that you need to know to pass the test. If you are particularly interested in an area, or feel that you want more information, do a quick search online. We've tried not to include too much depth in areas that are not as essential on the test. It is important to understand all major theories and concepts listed in the table of contents. It is also important to know any bolded words.

Don't worry if you do not understand or know a lot about the area. With minimal study, you can complete and pass the test.

One of the fallacies of other test books is test questions. People assume that the content of the questions are similar to what will be on the test. That is not the case. They are only there to test your "test taking skills" so for those who know to read a question carefully, there is not much added value from taking a "fake" test. So we have constructed our test questions differently. We will use them to teach you new information not covered in the study guide AND to test your knowledge of items you should already know from reading the text. If you don't know the answer to the test question, review the material. If it is new information, then this is an area that will be covered on the test but not in detail.

To prepare for the test, make a series of goals. Allot a certain amount of time to review the information you have already studied and to learn additional material. Take notes as you study; it will help you learn the material. If you haven't done so already, download the study tips guide from the website and use it to start your study plan.

Legal Note

All rights reserved. This Study Guide, Book and Flashcards are protected under US Copyright Law. No part of this book or study guide or flashcards may be reproduced, distributed or stored in a retrieval system, or transmitted in any form or by any means, electronic, mechanical, photocopying, recording, or otherwise, without the prior written permission of the publisher Breely Crush Publishing, LLC.

DSST is a registered trademark of The Thomson Corporation and its affiliated companies, and does not endorse this book.

FLASHCARDS

This section contains flashcards for you to use to further your understanding of the material and test yourself on important concepts, names or dates. Read the term or question then flip the page over to check the answer on the back. Keep in mind that this information may not be covered in the text of the study guide. Take your time to study the flashcards, you will need to know and understand these concepts to pass the test.

Absenteeism	**Act utilitarianism**
Affirmative action	**Alien Tort Claims Act**
Bipartisan Campaign Reform Act	**Body language**
Bribe	**Caux Round Table**

A person examines a situation, considers all the possible actions they could take and decides which one would end most favorably for all involved.	When an employee is chronically absent from work.
Allows foreign citizens to bring a citizen of the United States to trial in the United States.	Programs which seek to reduce or reverse the effects of past discrimination.
The way that people's bodies are used in communication, such as through gestures, poses or facial expressions.	(BCRA) Designed to limit the use of soft money in political campaigns.
A Swiss organization which works to create awareness in businesses and teaches strategies to maintain a minimum ethical standard.	An attempt to influence someone to make a decision they wouldn't normally make.

CEO	**CFO**
Child labor laws	**CIO**
Civil Rights Act	**Command and Control Regulation**
Conflict diamonds	**Conflict of interest**

Chief Financial Officer. Responsible for managing budgets, investments and financial goals.	Chief Executive Officer. Responsible for running the company, but must report to a board of directors.
Chief Information Officer. Responsible for managing a company's information systems.	Any law which regards the labor standards affecting persons under 18.
Regulations which dictate how a company should manage certain processes that pollute the environment.	Act which provides protection against discrimination.
When a person has multiple roles or interests which influence each other.	Diamonds which are mined and sold by groups or countries to fund insurrections.

| Consequentialism | Conventional morality |

| Cookie | Corporate social responsibility |

| Deontological ethics | Discrimination |

| Dukes vs Wal-Mart | Ecology |

A person's main goal is conforming to societal norms and values and bases morality on what is expected of them.	A term encompassing any moral theory which bases morality on the consequence of an action.
The consideration of large companies about the well being of society when they make business decisions.	Used to track a person's information and preferences while they are on the internet.
Treating a person differently on a basis of race, color, religion, gender or other factors.	Claims that the morality of an action is determined by the morality of the action itself – regardless of the consequence.
The interaction of people (and businesses) with the environment.	Dukes unsuccessfully attempted to sue Wal-Mart for discrimination against women.

Economical ethics

Economics

Enron

Environmental justice

Environmental Protection Agency

Environmental racism

Equal Employment Opportunity Commission

Ergonomics

The study of all of the markets over a particular geographic area.	Ethics regarding business and money related issues.
A move toward equality among all races in issues relating to environmental hazards.	Company which hid billions of dollars in debt through dishonest accounting practices.
When environmental hazards affect different races disproportionately.	(EPA) Works to protect workers through regulating environmental factors.
The study of designing more comfortably or easily used equipment.	A federal agency which investigates violations of the Civil Rights Act.

Espionage

Ethical egoism

Ethical relativism

Ethnicity

Facilitating payment

False Claims Act

Family interest

Federal Labor Standards Act

The belief that people should act only in their best interests.	When companies spy on each other.
Cultural origin.	The belief that ethics are a product of society, and are therefore determined by it.
Law which encourages whistle blowing on companies committing fraud against the federal government.	Another name for a grease payment.
Dictates child labor standards on the federal level.	When family interests come into play in business decisions. Such as hiring a family member.

Food and Drug Administration	**Foreign Corrupt Practices Act**
Glass ceiling	**Grease payment**
Hard money	**Hostile work environment**
In kind contribution	**Insider trading**

Law which makes it illegal for any US company to bribe foreign officials.	(FDA) A regulatory agency which was created to ensure public health and safety.
When a person pays a low level official of a foreign country to make something happen faster than it normally would.	An invisible barrier to the progress of women and minority groups.
Created in sexual harassment cases when an action is unwanted, severe and has an effect on the claimant's ability to work.	Money legally donated to a candidate used for the purpose of campaigning.
When a person trades stock when they have information not available to the general public which influences their actions.	When a person or company trades goods or services in place of money.

International Monetary Fund

Kantian ethics

Karen Silkwood

Kerr-McGee

Kimberly Process Certification Scheme

Kohlberg's Model of Cognitive Moral Sevelopment

Kyoto protocol

Labor unions

Determines the morality of an action based on the feasibility of applying it as a universal rule.	(IMF) An organization which has the responsibility of stabilizing international trade and preventing international trade crises.
A plant which produced plutonium pellets to fuel nuclear reactors.	An employee of Kerr-McGee who died suspiciously after investigating the plant's inadequate safety measures.
A six step model which describes the stages of human moral development.	Regulates the sale of diamonds to decrease the circulation of conflict diamonds.
A legal entity which bargains on behalf of employees to improve working conditions.	Legally binding agreement aimed at reducing worldwide greenhouse gas emissions.

Legal ethics

Living wage

Martha Stewart

Minimum wage

Ministerial conference

MNC

Morality

New social contract

A wage that is sufficient to allow education, reaction, health and eventually retirement.	Ethics regarding the actions of lawyers.
A government mandated standard of the lowest pay an employer can give an employee.	Arrested in 2001 for insider trading.
Multinational Corporation.	Conference held every two years which appoints a director of the WTO.
Employees are expected to increase their knowledge, improve over time, work their hardest and be loyal and ethical.	Used to describe a person's character, beliefs and how they will act or respond to different situations.

Noisy withdrawal

Non-disclosure agreement

North American Free Trade Agreement

Occupational Health and Safety Administration

Outside employment

Outsourcing

Philanthropy

Political action committees

An agreement between two or more groups to keep information private.	When a lawyer becomes aware of frauds committed by their client and withdraws legal representation for their client.
(OSHA) Works to protect workers against workplace hazards.	(NAFTA) An agreement signed between Canada, Mexico and the United States to lower trade barriers.
Outsourcing is when a company moves part of their business to another location (typically in another country).	Conflict of interest in which a person has multiple jobs and their interests conflict.
(PACs) Organized by special interest groups to raise money and support for political candidates or issues.	Giving back to the community.

Post conventional morality

Pre conventional morality

Predatory pricing

Price discrimination

Privacy Act 1974

Proprietary information

Pump and dump

Pure Food and Drug Act

A person is ruled by their own conscience and is motivated by an obligation to society. 	A person's main goal is survival and they consider morality in terms of rewards and consequence. 
When a company charges different amounts for a product in different situations. 	Providing goods at lower prices to drive competitors out of business and then raising the price. 
Information which a business wants kept private. 	Protects the privacy of individuals as it relates to the government's ability to gather information. 
Worked to counter diseases and sickness caused by low sanitation in food producing industries in 1906. 	When a broker owns securities, inflates the price and sells them before it goes back down. 

Quid Pro Quo

Rule utilitarianism

Sarbanes-Oxley Act

Secretariats

Self-dealing

Sexual harassment

Shoulder surfing

Social engineering

A person considers an action independently of a situation and determines whether or not it is moral as a rule.	Literally "something for something." When two groups or companies exchange things of value.
Three representatives comprising the governing body of NAFTA.	Act passed in 2002 which tightened accounting and auditing regulations.
Any repeated, unwanted behavior of a sexual nature.	Conflict of interest in which a person is part of both ends of a deal.
Similar to hacking, but with the focus on gaining information through interactions with people.	When a person looks over a person's shoulder to learn their passwords or other information.

Social ethics

Soft money

Spam

Special interest groups

Sustainable development

The customer is always right

Truth in advertising

Truth in lending

Money which is donated to political parties for party building purposes. 	Ethics regarding the ways that people interact with each other. 
(SIGs) Any group which uses involvement in politics to further their beliefs and positions. 	When a person (or business) sends out large amounts of electronic messages indiscriminately. 
A mentality in which the business puts the needs and wants of the customer first. 	Using resources responsibly so that current and future needs can be met. 
Protects borrowers by requiring that certain information be disclosed when a person is applying for a loan. 	Law stating that a company must have truthful advertisements. 

Tyco	US Foreign Corrupt Practices Act
USA PATRIOT Act	Virus
WARN Act	Whistle blowing
World Bank	World Trade Organization

A law which makes it illegal to a person to bribe a foreign official, or to further bribes while on US soil.	Company whose CEO and CFO were discovered stealing millions of dollars from them.
A piece of code which is used to disrupt computer function.	Allows the government a wide license to gather information in an attempt to protect against terrorism.
Exposing one's employer (or business) for willfully committing illegal or unethical acts.	Requires that employers give their employees 60 days notice before mass layoffs.
(WTO) Designed to eliminate barriers to trade on a global level and assist developing countries in their trade.	Has the responsibility of fostering economic development.